With Love from Bali

A Memoir

Stephanie Huff

The Pink Backpack Press
A Division of The Pink Backpack
www.thepinkbackpack.com

Library and Archives Canada Cataloguing in Publication
Huff, Stephanie
With Love from Bali: A Memoir
ISBN 978-1-0689540-0-9 (book)
ISBN 978-1-0689540-1-6 (e-book)
1. Huff, Stephanie–Travel–General
2. Travel–Asia–General
3. Travel–Asia–Southeast
I. Title II. Title: A Memoir

Cover Design by Stephanie Huff
First edition 2024

To my parents for making me,
to my nervous system for breaking me,
and to Bali for re-shaping me.

Contents

1

Prologue: A One-Way Ticket to Burnout

My eyes flick open to unfamiliar surroundings behind white, gauzy mosquito netting. I lay motionless like a starfish in bed, with beads of perspiration on my skin. An audible gurgling, squelching noise emanates from my bowels, as I gingerly turn on my side, curling into a protective ball.

As a world traveler, I'm no stranger to health ailments while on the road. I contracted amoebic intestinal parasites not once, but several times, while living in Tanzania, vomited on a hiking trail in Colombia, fainted in the security line at the Mumbai airport, and was the unfortunate recipient of sand worms in my leg on an ill-fated trip to South Africa. Let me tell you, the only thing worse than having uncontrollable, explosive, fever-inducing traveler's diarrhea, is to have it on a work trip with colleagues.

When you're that sick, notions of professionalism, politeness and any regard whatsoever for how you appear to others, goes out the window. In fact, you go feral. I reverted to neanderthal status, ambulating in a posture so hunched that my knuckles may have dragged on the ground if they weren't otherwise occupied, protectively clutching my belly. With long tresses of damp, sweat-soaked hair dangling in my face, I grunt in search of the nearest toilet (and evidently, knowledge of how to create fire).

I mistakenly thought years of world travel and living on the continent of Africa would strengthen my stomach, making me invincible to such incidents, yet I'm the only one of our group to get sick. I'm also severely burned out and if I'm being honest, my body has been giving warning signs of an impending collapse for months. Weeks away from finishing a one-year research contract on a global health project at a university in Ireland, our team traveled to Malawi where I'm currently bedridden.

I've slept for two days straight, only rousing to the occasional knock at my door from colleagues who kindly bring me water or plates of food that I leave untouched. When not sleeping, I lay motionless, staring at the ceiling lost in over-analytical thought, retracing a sequence of dramatic events that brought me to this wretched state in the first place.

At the end of February 2020, I defended my PhD dissertation in a tiny conference room on my university campus, which also happened to be in my hometown: London, Ontario, Canada. While I completed all ten years of my post-secondary schooling at the same university, a rather uncommon feat in the world of academia, I traveled abroad every chance I got. Fortunately for my meager student bank account, I had a knack for travel hacking.

I leapt at the opportunity to live in Tanzania for a year to conduct my doctoral project in partnership with a local women's rights organization. As my work came to completion and I returned to Canada to graduate, I wasn't sure what was next for me, but strongly sensed it wouldn't be in my hometown. I felt drawn elsewhere, as if invisible tethers to distant lands tugged on my heart.

A mere 10-days later, the world shut down. I was grounded for the foreseeable future—in my hometown, might I add—and for the first time in 5-years, I didn't have the rigid, external structure of my PhD program. I didn't know what to do with myself or what I even wanted to do. I felt lost and adrift, grasping for anything to throw myself into.

As a graduation gift to myself and to pass the time, I enrolled in a remote yoga teacher training program, where lessons were live streamed on Zoom from a yoga school in Bali. While it was chaotic from the start, most notably with the director accidently live streaming herself naked, I earned my 200-hour vinyasa yoga teacher certificate.

Naturally, as logic presides, instead of slowly gaining experience teaching yoga, I dove headfirst into the industry, opting to build an online yoga studio with teachers from around the world. For the record, I still think it was a brilliant idea in the context of global lockdowns: you could 'travel' to a class taught from Myanmar, India or Sri Lanka and try styles of yoga not as commonly offered in North America.

At the first sign of global travel reopening in autumn of 2020, I saw my chance to escape and relocated to the Greek island of Kythnos to continue working on my business. There, I launched The Akash Between (Sanskrit for 'the space between'), at which point I realized I was in way over my head. While I adored the creative process of building and branding my business, I was now singularly responsible for managing and financing a team of yoga teachers, all in different locations and time zones. My primary focus became selling memberships, but I despised sales. Our yoga students were mostly family members and friends, so while I made some revenue from their support, it wasn't enough to stay afloat.

As the year ended, so too did my 3-month visa in Greece. I impulsively booked a ticket back to the place that felt like a second home: Tanzania. I returned in January 2021 and quickly ran out of cash, forcing me to close my brand-new business by February. I was regretful, but also largely relieved. Looking back on this time, it's like a fever dream, almost as if it never happened.

Back in Tanzania, I stayed in a lovely lake-side town called Mwanza where I lived as a PhD student. I rented a cottage I could not afford on a lush compound with guava trees and mischievous monkeys.

To add to the chaos of my life at this time, I met Jason, a tour operator. He offered to take me on an all-expenses paid, two-week safari in exchange for media coverage on my travel blog, 'The Pink Backpack'. He joined me on the trip, where he requested I teach him everything I could about social media and online marketing. It was a fast-paced adventure from exploring the urban streets of Arusha, to game drives in National Parks and bush walks on foot led by the Maasai. I was enormously grateful for the experience, but the days were long and evenings even longer around a laptop. I returned to my cottage more energetically depleted than ever and not a cent richer.

I needed a job, ASAP.

I was fortunate to almost immediately land a one-year, entry-level researcher job with a University in Ireland. The role involved helping to analyze and write-up data from a large global health project operating in Uganda, Ghana and

Malawi. I was offered an enormous amount of flexibility at this time, as Tanzania was now a 'red zone' country, limiting most outbound travel beyond the continent of Africa. My options were: stay in Tanzania, join the team in Malawi, or relocate to Ireland when the borders opened.

I was residing in Tanzania on a tourist visa, meaning I had to exit and re-enter the country when the visa expired every 3-months. In pre-pandemic times, this was not an issue; I turned visa-runs into adventures. On one trip, I circumvented Lake Victoria by land, from Tanzania to Rwanda, Uganda and down through Kenya. As a PhD student, I did so many visa-runs I ran out of passport pages.

During those 'strange times' as we called them, entering a different country felt like playing a game of chess, except the rules were constantly changing. To renew my Tanzanian tourist visa, I got a PCR test and prayed the strict entry regulations would still be the same by the time my bus reached the border to a neighboring country. Then I'd declare my test results and pay for a visa on arrival, get a hotel for the night, and do the process all over again the next day to re-enter Tanzania for another 90-days.

The logistics were stressful and mentally exhausting. I was eligible for residency in Ireland through my new job, meaning no more visa runs, but I couldn't travel directly to Dublin from a 'red zone' country without enduring a mandatory 12-day hotel quarantine for a whopping 2000 euros. Due to the glaring negative number in my bank account, this was not an option at the time.

So, I found a loophole.

I could enter Ireland freely if I first spent two-weeks in a country which wasn't a red zone. Egypt was still accepting travelers from Tanzania and was not a red zone country. It would be far less expensive to stay there for two weeks prior to traveling to Ireland, than to go directly and pay for the hotel quarantine. I packed my things, said my goodbyes to friends in Tanzania, and booked a one-way ticket to Cairo.

You might see where this is going, dear reader.

Egypt was inevitably red zoned, and I ended up 'stuck' there for 2 months. You might be thinking this serves me right for trying to outsmart the system, and yes, you are correct. I was served a slice of humble pie.

I ended up falling in love with Egypt though. I stayed in the Sinai Peninsula on the Red Sea, where my days were spent working remotely from beachside cafes and scuba diving world renowned coral reefs. I would later wish I stayed put and continued working from Dahab, but I was determined to get to Ireland.

I held romanticized notions of what my new life would be like there (I can blame the novel and film 'P.S. I Love You' for that). I fixated on moving to Ireland as the solution to all my problems, yet my airy-fairy, 'everything will work out' mentality was not grounded in pragmatism.

When I finally entered Dublin in August 2021, my Irish fantasy quickly dissipated into the reality of a housing crisis and a backed-up immigration system. I arrived at the same time as everyone else waiting for the mandatory hotel quarantine rule to drop. Thousands of International students and foreign workers descended on the capital, competing for available housing and immigration appointments to process our respective permits.

The only lodgings I managed to secure was a dilapidated flat on top of a pub in Temple Bar. Every evening after work, I walked through the pub and climbed the back staircase, strapping on my noise canceling headphones to drown out the drunkards from the street below. You can only listen to 'what will we do with a drunken sailor' so many times before you fantasize about throwing a shoe (or a steel-toed boot) out the window.

My coping mechanism at the time was escapism: I'd hop on a plane at the first sign of discomfort or dissatisfaction, literally fleeing my problems. Now, it was unclear if I left the country, whether I could even get back in. Only several appointments were released each day on the immigration website at an indeterminate time. It was like trying to score a Taylor Swift concert ticket, requiring dedication to reloading the page over-and-over.

I distracted myself with bottomless pints of Guinness and by December, I was deeply depressed and still without an immigration appointment. It began to seem impractical to process residency for a country I wasn't thriving in. I gave up on my Irish dream and took a one-way flight back to Canada with my tail between my legs.

In the new year, I continued to work remotely from Canada when my team unexpectedly offered to pay for my flight back to Ireland—if I wanted to return, that is. Surprisingly, I responded with renewed optimism.

My toxic trait is rarely saying no to things, even if it makes no logical sense, and especially when it comes to travel. Perhaps I even considered it a chance at redemption: I would force myself to love Ireland. I boarded another one-way flight to Dublin in February of 2022, this time renting a room off a colleague in a lovely townhome within walking distance to work. During these final months of my research contract with the Irish University, our team took the trip to Malawi.

The morning birds chirp a melodic song, harmonized by the gurgling of my infirm intestinal tract. I'm in a hotel in Lilongwe, Malawi's capital city, willing myself to feel better before the series of international flights I'm scheduled to take the next day. With urgency, I leap out of bed, wincing and hobbling in pain to the bathroom before collapsing horizontally again.

On some level, the spontaneous illness that reduced me to a sweaty, immobile state for days, feels necessary. The way I've been living (to put it kindly) is unsustainable—but between you and I—my life is a hot mess. Perhaps the only way I'd slow down, is to fall so sick that I literally can't move.

A forced state of stillness.

The truth is my whimsical, free-spirited persona is feigned. I make it seem as if I'm living like this by choice, in pursuit of adventure, but I'm no longer in the driver's seat. I'm wandering in search of direction, constantly traveling and ironically, never truly arriving. I don't know what I want to do, or even where I want to base myself, so I've left major life decisions up to fate to negate my personal responsibility for long-term planning.

As random opportunities present themselves, I say "yes" without a second thought, rather than considering potential consequences of that "yes". While this type of radical optimism opened doors to amazing life experiences, ranging from the unique to downright bizarre, I must admit 'doing it for the plot' just isn't working anymore. I'm exceedingly exhausted, dysregulated, and living in survival mode where work tasks supersede my health.

Before the work trip to Malawi, I interviewed for another research job at the University of Limerick to avoid a gap in employment after my current contract ends. Yet, the thought of moving to Limerick and sliding into another intensive research project fills me with dread. I'm not even interested in the research topic, so why did I pursue it in the first place?

Perhaps I felt shame on some level, for having put myself out there with my yoga business, just for it to not work out. Maybe I felt as if I should take a more practical, safe route to make up for failing, or to avoid failure twice in a row.

Do I want this job, or is it what I feel I 'should' do?

Deep down, I already know the answer. So, as I lay there, feverish and clammy, I ask myself for the first time: "what do I want?"

I don't know.

You see, dear reader, I'm the type of person who learns by trial and error—unfortunately in my case—mostly by error. I'm consistently edging closer to notions of what I want, by learning the hard way, what I don't want. While my list of 'don't wants' has become long, I continue to search for what will bring me happiness. Perhaps in a bigger sense, it's a purpose I'm chasing, or connection I seek. Maybe it's spiritual nourishment, or just a feeling of 'aliveness' beyond the hamster wheel I find myself on.

"I want to go to Bali," a quiet, tentative inner voice whispers.

The familiar tug of the invisible tethers returns: a longing inexplicably pulling me to a place I've never been before.

"I will go to Bali and figure it out."

2

The Island of the Gods

"Is this the flight from Perth?" an older Aussie bloke asks, breaking me out of my jet-lagged trance. I'm standing near an empty conveyor belt in a sweltering, dark and slightly chaotic arrivals hall. The baggage carousels lack proper signage indicating originating flight numbers, prompting anxious passengers to pace up and down the terminal in a frenzy.

I look at him blankly, without a single thought behind my eyes as my brain cells fight valiantly to remember where I've just flown from. To my horror, I can't remember. I quickly glance around, affirming there are faces I recognize from my flight in my proximity.

"No, this isn't the flight from Perth," I reply, after a lengthy pause. We flew in from Singapore, which of course, I recall with ease as soon as he walks away with a puzzled look on his face.

My suitcase is a flamboyant pink shade, making it easy to spot when it eventually appears on the slowly circulating conveyor belt. I haul it onto its wheels and cautiously enter what resembles a mosh pit by the immigration desk: a faceless sea of bodies and luggage shrouded in darkness due to a power outage. I approach the immigration agent, armed with copies of travel documents, and he places a visa sticker in my passport.

I have six months in Indonesia.

I enter a brighter, winding labyrinth of currency conversion counters, food stalls and SIM card shops. A blast of warm, humid air hits me as I step outside and scan the crowd of patiently waiting taxi drivers with near-identical white signs. I spot a young Balinese man in a crisp white t-shirt with a flower in his hair, holding a sign for 'Stevani' and tentatively approach him. He smiles and authoritatively takes my bag. "Come, I am parked here."

I immediately relax and follow him to an air-conditioned SUV, where he tells me his name is Kedak. He looks to be in his early twenties and brightens when I share, I'm from Canada. "It's my dream to go there," he gushes, dreamily telling me of a guy from his village who works on a cruise ship that stopped in Vancouver[1].

The journey from I Gusti Ngurah Rai International Airport to Ubud takes us through the bustling urban streets of Denpasar, notorious for its dense, sprawling traffic. I don't mind and enthusiastically take in the sights from my passenger window. Sky-high statues tower over us from roadside monuments and central round-abouts, the latter serving as a haven for out-of-place pedestrians attempting to cross the multi-laned streets.

A line of motorbikes forms along the median, edging forward in unison like railcars on a train track. The more daring riders narrowly squeeze between moving vehicles, methodically honking to assert their presence. I'm both impressed and intimidated by the driving in Bali.

After two hours we arrive in the Penestanan Kaja village of Ubud, and Kedak eases the SUV down a narrow street which seems to abruptly end, converging into a sidewalk. A Balinese woman on a red moped awaits our arrival at the junction, expertly strapping my oversized suitcase on the back of her ride and whizzing away down the thin strip of concrete without a word. Within moments she's returned, motioning for me to get on the back. I offer Kedak four

[1]On my second visit to Bali, Kedak couldn't collect me from the airport because he was in Vancouver for his new job on a cruise ship. I was delighted for him, and we chuckled via WhatsApp over the irony that he was in my home country at the same time I arrived back in his.

100,000 rupiah banknotes and wave goodbye as I clumsily straddle the idling moped.

The cement track has sharp drop-offs on either side into adjacent rice fields, which are brimming with tall, delicate stalks rising from murky water. As an oncoming motorbike approaches, we slow to a crawl, inching forward so neither bike tumbles sideways into the tepid field. A farmer with knee-high rubber boots and a wide-brimmed hat wades through the crops, pausing to smile up at us. The track forks and we slowly turn at a precarious 90-degree angle onto an even thinner strip of concrete leading to a palm tree lined property.

I'm led down large stone steps to the studio apartment I've rented for a couple months. It has a funky open-air kitchen with a breakfast bar and a small bathroom area opening into a bedroom entirely enclosed by glass. Stepping stones wrap around the bedroom, leading to a koi pond and a thatch-roofed deck overlooking a lush ravine. The view is terrific: a panorama of ancient sky-high trees with dense leaves and long tendrils of vines swaying in the soft breeze.

The 'jungle deck' as I affectionately call it, was the selling feature for me when I booked the place, envisioning morning meditation and yoga in the ambiance of nature. What I hadn't fully considered, are the mosquitos. As I unpack and settle in, a cloud descends upon me, vehemently buzzing and nipping at my ankles. I imagine their little bug brains excitedly thinking "fresh meat!" as they drink my blood from miniscule salt rimmed and umbrella adorned cocktail glasses. Retreating to the safety of the bedroom, I examine the resulting blueberry-sized welts, before taking a hot shower and swiftly falling into a comatose sleep.

The next morning, I wake before my alarm goes off, not because I'm particularly well rested, but due to my insufferably itchy mosquito bites. I clamber out of bed and slide open the glass door to the outdoor kitchen to make a cup of tea, before relocating to the jungle deck. Music from a Gamelan instrument drifts through the trees from somewhere in the distance and a bat swoops overhead, gliding through a morning sky yet to fully illuminate.

A tiny thrill slides through me.

It's day one of my self-inflicted meditation regime, an ambitious one-hour session each morning. At least I have the foresight to apply mosquito spray before settling into a cross-legged position on the jungle deck. Eyes closed now, my body faces the ravine below. I can hear gentle babbling from the water, a chorus of morning songbirds, and a cloud of cicadas alerting me to the humidity of the day (as if I haven't noticed, I'm already glistening with sweat).

Nearly a decade before, I set out on a 3-month spiritual pilgrimage through India, traversing the country from South to North and visiting holy sites along the way. When I finally reached the staggering Himalayan mountains, I signed up for a silent meditation retreat at a Buddhist center in a tiny town called Dharamshala, home to the Dalai Lama after his exile from Tibet. It was there I learned how to meditate, or according to the Tibetan monks, 'how to tame my monkey mind'.

It's doubtful whether anything has been tamed in the years to follow, but I have experienced benefits from meditation, so I'm determined to get back into a dedicated routine. An hour each morning is not sustainable for me long-term, so I view my new routine as more of a 'mental bootcamp' to propel me into a healthier state of mind.

It quickly becomes apparent just how out of practice I am. My yappy mind conjures everything from decade old memories, to thoughts of what I might have for breakfast in the span of mere seconds. I catch myself veering off and swiftly return my focus to my breathing, counting[2] upwards on each exhale. I can barely make it to 10 breaths before I'm distracted and lose count, having to start all over again.

---

[2]Ānāpānasati, or 'mindfulness of breathing' is a Buddhist meditation teaching. The Tibetan Buddhist variation I learned during my silent retreat prescribes a counting exercise to assist the mind to concentrate on the breath. Each inhalation and exhalation are counted as one, upwards to twenty-one, before starting over again.

Back at the Tibetan Buddhist center in India, one particularly stern monk taught us our minds are like dumpsters, presumably filled with garbage. We sat before her, cross-legged like children, diligently listening as she listed all the ways we were full of shit (my words, not hers) and how our contaminated minds were the cause of our own suffering (her words, not mine).

"Meditation is like taking out the trash in your mind," she barked in a thick German accent.

I quite like this metaphor and eventually give up on my counting exercise to simply observe the state of my dumpster and its contents: it's of landfill proportions.

When my timer indicates 60-minutes have passed, I gingerly stretch my stiff and numb limbs, proud of my efforts of 'garbage disposal' duty. The sun is now high in the sky and my next thought rolls in instantaneously: coffee.

3

Snap, Crackle, Pop

I retrace my way down the narrow concrete track, on foot this time, taking caution to avoid stepping on the gorgeous offerings laid out in front of doorways I pass. I would later learn these tiny square parcels filled with flowers, rice and lit incense sticks are called 'canang sari', a daily ritual for purification, spiritual protection and harmony.

I notice floral designs painstakingly etched into concrete, butterflies gliding through lush foliage, and fallen white flowers sprinkling my path. I slow to collect one in my fingers and smell its fragrance, placing it in my hair. Occasionally, a motorbike rounds the bend, and I step aside while trying not to tumble into the rice paddies.

Eventually I reach the road and walk through the village, which is now bustling with activity. Temple tops peak over tall gates leading to family compounds and Warungs—locally owned shops and restaurants—mark every corner. An elderly woman marches purposefully with a walking stick taller than her body and street dogs sleep lazily in the shade. Several Balinese men who sit together, leisurely chatting and smoking, casually offer me a ride.

"Taxi miss?"

I politely decline, turning into a local restaurant called 'Warung Ting Ting'.

I order Balinese kopi, a small cup of coffee the strength of rocket fuel with a bottom layer of thick, sludgy grounds, and Nasi Goreng, a plate of vegetarian fried rice topped with an egg. My food comes with a tiny dish made from folded banana leaf containing sambal, a red sauce I impulsively dump onto my rice before tasting it. I quickly realize my mistake: it's spicy!

Scrolling the map on my phone as I eat, I look for interesting landmarks in the area. Instead, I notice several spas advertising traditional Balinese massage and my interest peaks.

Nearly a decade prior, I sustained whiplash injuries to my neck in not one, but two, fender benders in the span of a year, pushing my neck to the point of no return. In addition to my 'mental bootcamp', I decide to do a complete overhaul of my health while in Bali. I'm long overdue for a generalized check up with a doctor, and my neck could use some serious TLC.

I decide on a spa with glowing reviews within walking distance called 'Starchild', positioned up a steep driveway off the main road in Penestanan. Behind the front desk, there's a lovely garden with a babbling fountain and side-by-side rooms with massage tables and large jacuzzi tubs. I'm led by a Balinese woman to a room and instructed to place my clothes in a woven basket on a shelf.

Unsure of the massage etiquette here in Bali, I whisper to her, "Do I leave my undergarments on?"

Nonchalantly, she tells me to take everything off and lay under the sarong. She gestures to the vibrant, floral patterned cloth on the bed, before exiting to offer me privacy.

I strip down to my underwear, opting to leave them on for modesty purposes, and clamber onto the massage table, awkwardly flipping onto my stomach to fit my face into a cushioned cut-out. I layer the sarong over my back, just as she knocks and re-enters the room.

I'm not sure what I expected, but not in my wildest imagination, did I anticipate her climbing up onto the table to straddle me. She works her elbows into my sore back muscles, prompting bizarre facial expressions I'm grateful no one can see. She repositions herself directly on top of me, allowing the full weight of her body to settle over my legs and back, cueing an audible crack of my taught spine.

Snap, crackle, pop.

Her kneecaps pushing into my back is slightly painful, which is somehow funny in juxtaposition to the whale sounds now emanating from the speaker tucked in the corner. I think whale sounds are supposed to be relaxing in a primal sort of way, but they've always made me imagine over-sized, underwater ghosts. Unfortunately, I'm now reminded of this and fight off heaving, body-shaking giggles.

"Are you ok?" she asks, with concern as she gets down from the table.

"Yes, thank you, so relaxing," I reply, while simultaneously questioning my choice of adjectives.

She folds down the sarong and tucks it into my butt crack. My undergarments have probably disappeared altogether, shoved so far up my nether regions I must perform my meditative counting exercise to restrain the immature hysteria bubbling up.

I guess that's one way to make sure the sarong doesn't slip down.

Next, she works my legs, taking each ankle backwards towards my head. My back arches to accommodate the severe stretch until eventually, I resemble a glistening hog-tied swine. When it's time for me to flip over, I'm surprised by my first ever stomach massage, a rather ticklish endeavor.

The session ends at my scalp with karate chops to my skull. At this rate, I imagine her job could almost be stress relieving, like going to one of those rage rooms designed for smashing glass with a baseball bat, except it's an annoying tourist getting beat up.

I wobble home, feeling unstable on my feet as my muscles and joints are unfamiliarly loose. Within a few hours, tiny fingerprints form on my body like purple dalmatian spots, and I scuttle around my jungle flat in pain, hunched over like Quasimodo.

While I can confidently confirm I'm not a sadomasochist, I enjoyed the massage, which seemed to lessen the golf-ball sized knots in my back. By the next morning, I feel lighter and immediately book my next session.

4

Serendipitous Greetings

I'm reading about the phenomenon of awakenings.

Awakenings emerge from a state of turmoil, sorrow or suffering and often result in a spiritual outcome: a crumbling of one's identity or belief systems, or a renewal of hope and faith. They open us to the awareness that we are more than our bodies; we have a soul, spirit, or consciousness, and we are connected to something greater than ourselves.

People from all over the world come to Bali during their own awakening, in pursuit of spiritual nourishment. Some say the island is magical, with palpable healing energy. There's even a legend passed around by new-age spiritual tourists, which says Bali reflects your own energy back to you. If there are things you're not dealing with in your life, it will force you in ways which can be—well, forceful.

Documented narratives from the first wave of hippies to come to the island in the 1970s relay jarring experiences where major life lessons were learned 'the hard way' following personal disasters or near-death experiences. Others recount coming to the island and unintentionally finding their soulmate or a new-found home. In other words, profound growth and healing just might be possible on the Island of the Gods, through ease or a universal face-plant.

After just a few weeks in Bali, I'm starting to feel better physically and mentally and have a renewed sense of child-like joy and wonder. Maybe Bali really is a magical place, I think while reflecting on the words of a hippy I met at a cafe the other day: "The energy here is powerful, it's like a vortex.[3] It can elevate you to new heights or suck you up and spit you back out."

I don't know much about vortexes, but I did feel an inextricable pull to come here, and I'm open to whatever, or whoever might cross my path.

Today I'm meeting an Australian woman named Karen for lunch at a popular vegan restaurant called Alchemy.

---

[3]Bali is positioned at the intersection of two 'Ley lines', which supposedly encircle the planet and connect prominent landmarks. According to New Age Spirituality, these lines create an energetic grid or a 'vortex' where they cross paths, amplifying the energy of a particular place—if you believe in that kind of thing.

Karen reached out to me on a pet sitting platform I periodically use to find house sits. The app connects pet owners needing someone to watch their animals while they are away, with travelers who stay in their homes for free in exchange for animal care. What started as a way for me to escape my wretched pub-top flat in Dublin, has since turned into one of my top travel hacks for finding free accommodation while on the road. Karen needs a dog sitter, so she suggests lunch at a dog-friendly establishment as a 'meet and greet' with her two poodles.

Karen is a stunningly gorgeous middle-aged woman with glowing skin, blue eyes set behind long lashes, bouncy chestnut curls and legs for days. She confidently strolls into the cafe barefoot in daisy duke denim shorts and a tank, leading her two white poodles to the lounge area where I'm already seated.

She introduces me to Bunny, a chunky creature more closely resembling a baby lamb than a poodle, and Bella, a delicate toy-sized dog that could comfortably fit in my purse. We sit on a couch and chat over salad bowls with the 'girls' at our feet. Soon enough, they hop up onto the couch and rest their heads directly in my lap. Karen beams and claps in delight. It seems I have the girls' approval. We exchange phone numbers and hug goodbye.

After lunch, fatigue hits me like a category 5 hurricane and I decide to take a motorcycle taxi home through a ride share app called 'Gojek'. While I stand out front waiting for my driver to pull up, I notice a man standing to the side, glancing at his phone.

He's hard to miss: tall, dark and handsome in an Earthy, bohemian sort of way. He has brown wavy hair that's neither groomed nor disheveled, but effortlessly wind swept. His dark eyes periodically glance up at me from his phone as we wait there, together but not together.

"Are you waiting for a ride?" I ask.

His smile seems to rest in satisfaction that I broke our silence first.

"I'm waiting for a delivery actually, how about you?"

I confess I'm headed home, still exhausted from my recent travels to get here.

Tall, dark and handsome: "Ahh you've just arrived! Where are you from?"

He seems to noticeably perk up when I share, I'm Canadian.

"Ohhh, Canada. You have a good reputation." he says with a wink.

"I'm French. I've been traveling for a few years, lived in Australia for ten, but I was always coming here so eventually I just moved over…I'm Claude by the way."

He extends his hand, and I accept, simultaneously fighting the impulse to croon, "enchanté." Instead, I reply, "I'm Steph, nice to meet you."

As if on cue, my motorcycle taxi pulls up and I say something along the lines of, "well that's me," as I climb on the back of the bike. The driver makes a slow arch to turn around and I glance back, locking his eyes.

"Bye," I call out to him, smiling mischievously.

Still inflated from my flirtatious encounter with tall, dark and handsome (TD&H), I download a dating app later that evening. I've been hopelessly single for two years by now, never quite staying in one place long enough to form meaningful connections. I figure it's about time to 'get back out there'. Splayed out on my stomach across my bed, I create a profile and swipe through an array of singles on my phone.

My hand pauses, hovering over the screen. I can't believe my eyes, it's him: TD&H! He looks at me from the screen through long lashes some girls pay good money for. Without hesitation, I swipe right to indicate my interest and it's an instant match.

"So, we meet again." I playfully type into the message box.

I can see three little dots hovering as he immediately writes a response.

"Sorry, but have we met?"

Ohhh…he doesn't recognize me.

Disappointment rises within me, and I anxiously wonder if my profile photos don't reflect how I look in real life? I mean, it is quite humid in Ubud after all, resulting in a gleam on my skin that's less of a fresh, dewy look and more of a moist glistening of the upper lip. My normally straight hair is frizzy here, and wearing makeup is pointless because it just drips down my face like a wax figurine melting into a grotesquely deformed shape.

My mind catastrophizes this information into a horrific thought.

Am I unintentionally cat-fishing men on the internet?

No, I reassure myself.

When we met earlier, I looked cute in a casual sort of way, dressed in beige linen pants, paired with a simple black tank top and a high ponytail with loose, blonde tresses framing my face. I must have misconstrued the flirtatious interaction. Maybe he was just being polite, so it was not so memorable to him.

"We met standing outside of Alchemy, didn't we? Otherwise, you have a twin walking around Ubud."

I continue to ruminate, feeling hopelessly awkward until my phone pings with a reply.

"I live in Canggu…send him my regards, he's very good looking."

Oh my god. It's not even the same guy.

I'm the kind of person who forgets a name 2.5 seconds after it's told to me; it's in one ear and out the other. I forgot the Frenchman's name within moments of him uttering it, so his twin's name (which does sound rather Italian for the record) didn't prompt a swift realization that he's a different man altogether.

"Why am I so awkward?" I whisper, to no one in particular, as I groan softly and drop my face to my hands. I close the app and switch off my phone for the night.

5

A Recipe for Disaster

When I first began solo traveling as a young adult, it was before the days of 'pay-as-you-go' SIM cards and Wi-Fi signals nearly everywhere. I'd buy a burner phone and frequent internet cafes for my basic communication needs. Without cellular data to use Google Maps or to email updates to family, I was chronically lost and digitally disconnected.

The result was countless requests that I start a blog, so folks back home could follow my adventure. This was an ironic suggestion since my primary issue was a lack of internet, but the idea resonated with me. In 2016, 'The Pink Backpack' travel blog was born. My website has since turned into a small business, connecting me to people all over the world, including other business owners who occasionally invite me to review their travel products and services.

I took a hiatus from my blog during my chaotic time in Ireland, but here in Bali, a spark of inspiration returns. I begin posting on social media with renewed passion and even begin dabbling in food photography.

One afternoon, while wandering down Raya Ubud Street to take in the sights, such as the nearby Ubud Palace, I stop for lunch at 'Casa Luna'. I snap a photo of my aesthetically plated meal: a tangerine-hued glass of Jamu—a turmeric herbal drink—and a rainbow salad, posting it to my Instagram account. This spontaneous decision would prove to be serendipitous, leading to a media invitation from Casa Luna to return for a complimentary meal, a cooking class and two nights at their family-owned guesthouse around the corner.

I immediately agree.

A few days later, I return to the lower level of Casa Luna to participate in a cooking class on vegan food as plant medicine. Spread across the rectangular table, are an array of fresh ingredients, cooking utensils and a recipe for 'banana flower curry'.

Our group is hosted by a spritely and vivacious older Balinese woman who introduces each ingredient one-by-one, along with its healing properties and medicinal uses. I'm particularly interested in two ingredients I'm seeing for the first time: galangal, a knobby root similar to ginger and known to be anti-inflammatory, and the banana flower, which can promote anxiety reduction.

Just what the doctor ordered.

I examine the banana flower and snap a photo while ironically sipping an iced americano, a proven catalyst for my over-active, anxious thoughts.

Our leader demonstrates how to mince cloves of garlic and finger-like chunks of ginger, prompting an array of clumsy chopping and audible giggles from the all-female group. She even takes one for the team and handles all the turmeric root so we won't stain our fingernails a vibrant shade of yellow (though I can't say the same for my mouth after impulsively tasting a hunk).

The cooking takes place at a second table, where we gather around a wok-like basin. We each throw in our ingredients, which sizzle and steam in hot coconut oil like a bubbling cauldron.

Eventually the recipe comes to life, and we plate up rice topped with a fragrant curry. We heartily tuck in, generously spooning mouthfuls between pleasant chit-chat.

I learn most of my companions are in Bali on holiday, no longer than a couple of weeks, so I receive a few raised eyes and envious responses when I share, I've come for six months.

"Wow, I'm so jealous!" one Australian lady tells me.

"My daughter is about your age, and she loves to travel too."

After finishing our lunch, we clap for our host and thank her for a lovely class. I briefly meet the owner, the author of a Bali-based memoire I coincidentally picked up at a bookshop down the road, but I wouldn't make the connection until after I read it weeks later.

I return to Raya Ubud Street and turn left up a steep hill towards 'Honeymoon Guesthouse', where I'm looking forward to a change of scenery for a couple nights. The guesthouse appears to be inside a traditional Balinese compound with its own temple. I patiently wait at the front desk behind an older American woman, who's desperate for the Wi-Fi password, intentionally adding with a condescending tone: "I asked for it earlier, but they didn't bring it…like most things here."

Instinctively, my eyes widen in shock at the unnecessary rudeness. The American lady stomps off, with a slip of paper containing the Wi-Fi details in hand and I approach the desk. The young receptionist appears to be entirely unphased.

They must be used to this entitled behavior.

Unfortunately, some travelers come to Bali expecting carbon-copy versions of the establishments they're used to back home, or with the notion that rules all together do not exist. Copious tourists on motorbikes drive arrogantly, perpetually in a rush while failing to wear helmets. Expat influencers show off beach clubs[4], iced matcha lattes and cold plunges after a gym pump, as if trying to emulate Los Angeles or Byron Bay lifestyles, rather than Balinese ones.

The receptionist leads me to a suite garnished with ornate wood furnishings, intricately carved and delicately inscribed. The four-post canopy bed with mosquito netting looks fit for a Queen, so regal it could be something out of a scene from Bridgerton. The bathroom is intentional in its design, bringing elements of the garden inside with large, shuttered windows opening outwards into lush foliage.

After capturing images and videos to share with the owners, I settle onto the lounge chair on my private terrace and swipe open my phone. There are several notifications from the dating app, which I'm hesitantly using after noticing most of the men fall within distinct categories.

First, there's the party boy: when he's not at the club or behind a DJ booth, he's catching waves. He lives in Canggu, or he's there on holiday 'for a good time, but not a long time'. There's a 9.5/10 chance he's barefoot and shirtless, even

---

[4]Years later, I read a news clip citing a new nickname for Canggu: "Little Moscow", inciting anger and concern from locals over Bali losing its cultural identity and sparking a debate as to whether foreign investment is causing more harm than good. Tourism is a massive industry in Bali, but just like anything in life, there are pros and cons.

while driving his motorcycle: no shirt, no shoes, will provide service.

There are the swingers, a package deal searching for their third to spice up their open marriage, and 'old man river' who's come to Bali to rediscover himself (which is all fine and dandy, except for the blatant 'under exaggeration' of his age, which I can tell on account of his profile photo being a photo of an actual printed photo).

Finally, and most notably in Ubud, there's the guru: he's spiritually 'woke' and wants everyone to know about his state of enlightenment. He's most likely a podcast host, life coach or intimacy 'expert'.

There is also the matter of representation: almost everyone is white. Where are the Balinese men, or men of color at all?[5] Language settings might have something to do with the lack of Indonesian profiles, as I assume the algorithm would only show me those set up in English. While for some, not having a smartphone would prevent using the app entirely.

Even among the tourists and expats though, the profiles are not very diverse, nor are the visitors wandering around for that matter.

---

[5]This was experienced in 2022, a few months after Bali re-opened its borders to international tourists. Tourism had not fully recovered and the number and diversity of visitors at the time reflected this. The dating landscape could be vastly different now, but I cannot speak to this as I've permanently sworn off all dating apps.

At the same time, I'm desperate for connection. My new health regime means I'm abstaining from alcohol, but learning how to socialize and date without it is new to me: I'm more reserved and socially awkward. It's far outside my comfort zone to approach a stranger to introduce myself, so making new friends is proving to be a challenge. For now, a dating app seems to solve this issue, offering an instant way to meet people—albeit only men—and arrange social outings.

My first date doesn't seem to fit into one of the categories. Tim is 6 foot 4 with long, blonde wavy hair, blue eyes and bronzed skin: he's the quintessential Australian surfer dude.

Australian men have a reputation in Bali of being boisterous Bogans[6], but Tim seems well-spoken and intellectual. We chat back and forth on the app, and he shares he's an environmental scientist. I'm intrigued and reminded not to judge a book by its cover.

Tim offers to drive an hour from Canggu to Ubud to meet me, tampering his enthusiasm with the excuse, "I haven't been to Ubud in ages!"

He's late after having to switch guesthouses last minute and I'm beginning to go stir crazy waiting for him, so I relocate to a cafe and order a smoothie bowl. Tim eventually meets me there, but after an hour driving his bike in the

---

[6]A Bogan is an obnoxious, barefoot, and most likely drunk person that can be found at Finns Night Club or in the Canggu area in general.

midday sun, he appears to be overheated: his face is tomato red, and his clammy arms feel damp to the touch when he greets me with a hug.

He grabs a coconut water from the self-serve refrigerator and takes a long pull from the cool glass bottle. I notice a large sweat stain on the front of his shirt and suggest we go for a swim. The guesthouse has a lovely, shared pool, which I noticed hardly anyone using, so I'm willing to wager we'd have the space to ourselves.

Tim is a true surfer, conveniently wearing swim trunks, so naturally he agrees to this idea. I hop on the back of his bike and direct him to the location.

Our conversation is light and easily flows as we intermittently cool off in the pool. Just as our banter is becoming increasingly flirtatious, Tim's demeanor changes. Rather urgently, he asks if he can use my bathroom.

"For sure, my key is just there on the lounger," I reply, gesturing to the direction of my room.

He grabs the key and excuses himself, and I return to my lounge chair in the sun.

Approximately twenty minutes pass and I begin to worry. *Did I just get ghosted? Or worse, robbed? Or even worse yet, has he clogged my toilet?*

I collect my things and nervously approach the room, but see it's still securely locked with no Tim in sight. Returning to the pool, I'm confused and slightly worried after checking the time: it's been 45 minutes.

Eventually Tim returns, ghostly pale and looking embarrassed.

"Are you okay? I went to my room to check on you but couldn't find you."

"Hey sorry, I'm not feeling so hot. I found a bathroom around the other side of the pool," he sheepishly tells me.

I read between the lines Tim didn't want to destroy my bathroom and approach the matter of his digestive tract with delicacy.

Tim divulges he felt a wave of dizziness and nearly passed out, which was what took so long. I feel horrible for him and ask if he'd like me to get anything from a pharmacy.

He pauses, looking mortified before replying with a dejected look. "Yes please, maybe Motilium?"

I suggest he stays in my room to rest while I walk to the pharmacy. Speed-walking down the lane towards the main road, I simultaneously google Motilium, a brand of medicine I've never heard of. My search results confirm what I already suspected: Tim has diarrhea.

I enter 'Guardian', a chain of pharmacies dispersed around the island, and select Motilium, rehydration salts, and a large bottle of water. After denying an onslaught of attempted upsells of digestive related products, like charcoal and probiotics, I pay and make my way back to my waiting patient.

I find Tim resting on the bed, resembling a pale corpse: eyes closed and laying on his back, his hands are neatly folded across his chest.

"Tim?" I cautiously whisper.

Without moving, he flicks open his eyes and glances at me still standing in the doorway. I slowly approach the bedside and hand him the pharmacy bag, which he accepts gratefully. Struggling to sit upright, he takes cautious sips of the cold water before downing two tablets. I help by mixing the rehydration salts into the bottle and hand it back.

Some color begins to return to his cheeks, and he apologizes profusely for ruining the date before making an excuse to get back to Canggu before sundown. I reassure him he doesn't have to rush off if he's still dizzy, wanting to make sure he's safe to drive, but the poor soul is mortified no doubt and makes a swift exit.

Needless to say, we did not see each other again.

It was rather 'shitty' as far as first dates go.

6

A Psychic

I decide to attend a yin yoga class with live music at the suggestion of Matt, an American expat living in Ubud. We matched on the dating app, but haven't met in person yet, so he suggests I join him at the class.

Naturally, I'm running late and anxiously clutching the back of a racing Gojek bike, which weaves in and out of dense traffic. My driver swiftly delivers me up a steep driveway to the winding entrance of the 'Yoga Barn'. I can hardly describe the place as a yoga studio. It's more of a hub with multiple shalas, a cafe, spa and lounge areas. At any hour from dawn till dusk, there are numerous classes, workshops and events going on.

I pay for a drop-in class at the front desk and wait in a crowd of spandex-clad bodies hovering beneath a spiral staircase. Realizing with relief I'm not late after all, I notice a rope blocking off the stairs to the loft studio. When it's removed, eager first timers rush forward like punks in a mosh pit.

I tip-toe barefoot up the winding staircase to a large, open-air loft, hesitating at the entrance to look for Matt. Some people are excitedly running to claim spots near the front, while others with phones glued to hands, film panoramic videos of the room. I turn my head away, as one girl brazenly passes her phone directly in front of my face.

Picking a space towards the back, I settle onto a blue yoga bolster, continuing to glance around the room. Instead of finding Matt, I notice Karen. She's looking glamorous as ever in a billowy, floor-length skirt, a woven crop top and a bedazzled skull cap, the kind a fortune teller might wear. She's accompanied by an older man, bald and smiling, in an unbuttoned linen shirt revealing a beaded mala necklace. They approach the front and greet the band members in tightly pressed hugs, claiming VIP spots which were saved for them.

The class is simply lovely. The teacher is a magnetic, dread-locked, Latino man with a gentle voice, offering a series of guided, slow-moving poses to invite rest and release. Alongside the poses, which we hold for extended periods of time, singers serenade us with beautiful siren-like vocals. I'm energized and enthralled by the experience.

Karen and her man-friend hang around chatting with the band after class, so I pop over to say hello. She introduces me to Anders, the older gentleman who I now assume is her partner, and their young British friend Xavier.

They plan on having dinner at a nearby restaurant and Karen invites me to join. I've still not spotted Matt, nor received any communication from him, so I accept her offer. I follow the group to Karen's red 4-door sedan, and we relocate to a raw vegan restaurant called 'Sayuri Healing Foods'.

Low and behold, who do I see when I walk in, but Matt. The man does a visible double take when he sees me. Now changed from my yoga clothes, I wear a flowy, floor-length sundress in a soft blue floral pattern. I'm barefoot, having left my sandals at the door, and my humidity-induced waves frame my post-yoga glowing face. He rises and gives me an awkward hug, sheepishly admitting he'd fallen asleep and missed the class.

"I just texted you back," he offers, a condolence to remedy his absence to an outing that was his suggestion in the first place.

Of course, the only vacant table is directly beside Matt's, so after introducing him to my new crew, they invite him to join us.

"So, how did you two meet?" asks Anders.

There's nothing more awkward than admitting to having met someone on a dating app. It seems to either prompt a pitying expression that one would have to resort to using a dating app in the first place or render assumptions of casual hook-ups. The reality is, meeting people 'in the real world' can be hard, especially for nomads. Dating apps, for better or worse, solve this problem, instantaneously connecting an array of romantic options right at one's fingertips. Matt must have felt equally as awkward because he merely offers, "we met online."

Anders changes the topic, "Xavier was just telling us he's a gifted energy channeler."

I'm unsure what this means, but I'm intrigued and take Xavier in fully for the first time: he's tall, towering over 6 feet, with blonde hair and blue eyes rimmed in round frames. In a posh British accent, he shares he often receives 'downloads' of information telepathically, within his mind.

"Where do you receive this information from?" I inquire.

As a PhD student and postdoctoral researcher, I was academically trained to question everything with a healthy dose of skepticism, examining theories from all sides to uncover correlations or gaps. It's a tendency I now struggle to switch off in everyday life, even in casual conversations.

I quickly add, "I mean, which energy are you connecting with? God, or a deity perhaps?"

There's a suspended pause at the table as he contemplates my questions. Instead of replying, he suddenly turns his body towards me, looking directly into my eyes.

"Do you have any Celtic connections? I see you running through a forest. It feels like olden days, it feels Celtic."

I'm surprised and momentarily rendered silent, while mentally grasping for any Celtic connection I might have.

I offer, "I do have Celtic ancestry, and I've just come from living in Ireland."

Karen and Anders make a collective 'oooohhh' in affirmation, as if we'd just cracked his coded message. Xavier quickly rebounds to add in, "Well, I usually get more detailed information in quieter, more private environments. We'd have to meet up another time for me to give you a better channeled message."

The night ends with solidified plans for me to house sit for Karen and Anders. They've planned a weekend in Uluwatu, an area boasting turquoise waters and pristine beaches in southern Bali, to celebrate Anders' 70th birthday.

I privately recoil in shock at his age: the man looks decades younger with glowing glass-like skin, clear twinkling eyes, and ample biceps. As for Matt, he excused himself from our table earlier, promising to 'catch me later', though I'm questioning whether I want to be caught by him at all after he ghosted me earlier.

As I prepare to take a Gojek home from the restaurant, Anders pipes up with a conspiratorial smirk on his face.

"Xavier, you're headed her way to Penestanan aren't you?"

"I am, do you fancy a lift Steph?"

Why do I get the feeling I've been set up?

I end up on the back of Xavier's bike, whipping through the cool night towards the rice paddies. I direct him past Warung Ting Ting to where the lane converges into the narrow cement track. He slows to a stop; there's no lighting, so the cement track looks particularly daunting in the dark.

"Jesus."

"I can walk from here, it's no problem."

"No, this looks too dark for you to walk alone, don't worry Steph."

He edges the bike forward along the sidewalk-width path, not exactly teetering but also not exuding confidence either. When I tell him to make the sharp 90-degree angle turn onto the even more narrow trail, he curses under his breath again.

"Christ, look at this one! No wonder you haven't got a scooter yet."

I giggle in response and hop off the bike when we reach the parking area of my jungle flat.

During our drive, Xavier mentioned a healer he worked with called Jewel who previously helped him overcome burnout. Now that he's stationary, I ask for more details.

"Actually Steph, you have a similar frequency as her. Angel energy. You would benefit from a session, I'll text you her details."

My ego is caught between flattery and eye-rolling cynicism, but I take him up on his offer and give him my number.

"Thanks for the drive home, Xavier. Goodnight."

Later, Karen would privately divulge a pattern she noticed. Xavier only seemed to receive 'energetic transmissions' for beautiful young women. Many women flock to Bali to heal from their respective traumas and heartaches and are potentially in vulnerable mental states. It's rather convenient he only gravitates to them, stressing if they're open to receiving personalized psychic messages, he would 'meet them privately' to act as a channel. I can see how his proposition works because it successfully captured my attention at dinner.

The predatorial 'guru archetype' is rampant[7].

Needless to say, I don't meet him for a private channeling, but do take his advice and book a healing session with Jewel.

---

[7]The predatorial guru is not unique to Bali. One of the founding gurus of the ashram I visited in India was later accused of sexual abuse. By then, he had passed away and could not be brought to justice. It's questionable whether there would be justice though, as the disbelief and victim blaming within the ashram was thick. The community came together to ostracize the victim and side with the guru, upholding their belief system and faith in the two-faced man they committed to follow.

Jewel no longer lives in Bali but offers 'energy healing' over the phone. I'm skeptical but book a session with her before my logical mind can say no. A few days later she calls, and I sit on my bed while she 'tunes in' to my energy. I tell her about my recent struggles with burnout and feeling highly sensitive to my environment and those around me, leading to a constant state of overwhelm.

"I'm sure you've heard of a spiritual empath before. You're quite gifted, I can tell, especially in the heart chakra, it's wide open."

I have heard of an empath before and relate to the concept of being able to perceive the emotions and energies of those around me.

However, I'm also aware of the psychological explanation of being an empath. The ability to 'read' people is a result of living in a chronic state of vigilance. When the fight or flight mode is continually activated, it becomes a habitual or intuitive psychological response to scan the environment and people in it for signs of impending danger or violence. It's literally a survival response.

I don't say this to Jewel though.

She asks if I have a pen and paper nearby and has me draw a dial, similar to the face of a clock.

"This is like your spiritual volume button. When you feel overwhelmed by your empath gift, you can psychologically turn down the dial or switch it off."

If only it were that easy.

Jewel tells me she can sense I have a special connection with animals and trees.

"If you aren't already communicating with them, you will be able to."

She has me draw two extra dials, one for animal communication and one for the trees.

"The trees[8] want to be a part of your healing. I'm hearing this strongly. The next time you find a tree, just go and wrap your arms around it."

Jewel completes the call with a 'light language' transmission meant to energetically heal me through sound frequencies. I listen in silence with curiosity as she speaks in a 'galactic dialect' resembling whispered gibberish. I wait for an incandescent light to surround my body, or to feel a powerful burst of pure love, but I don't.

I don't feel anything.

---

[8]Interestingly, just a year later I found myself living in a tree planting camp in Canada, where I single handedly planted nearly 100,000 trees. Tree planting is a solitary seasonal job which is incredibly challenging but can also be cathartic. While I'm not sure the trees 'healed me', the experience itself was powerful and transformative.

7

Nasi Campur is Cheaper than Therapy

I arrive shortly before a one-hour 'heart opening meditation' class at the Yoga Barn and join a crowd of waiting students outside the studio. The area is so packed with linen clad bodies, it resembles a mosh pit. New arrivals join the 'pit' and hover inches behind me, breathing moist air onto my neck. I'm already warm from the humidity, but in my claustrophobic discomfort, an additional heat radiates from my insides. Instinctually, I inch forward for some relief from the mouth breathers, but they eagerly claim this space too and the mob tightens.

I squirm through the sea of sunburned and sweaty skin towards empty space near the gift shop, gulping breaths of fresh air. A young Balinese woman now stands in the studio doorway and announces the room is ready.

"No phones are allowed in the studio please. No filming."

Eager attendees push forward and the crowd surges toward the girl, who leaps out of the way. I stand back and watch with perplexion of such aggressive behavior enroute to a meditation class.

One girl gets through the door and takes off running in hot pursuit of the best spot, dashing around slower moving students. Her toe catches on the edge a yoga mat and she launches forward, righting herself before tumbling onto the hardwood floor. She places her mat front and center, while I move to the periphery of the room, as far from her as possible.

Running girl now stands in front of the teacher's mat, which is adorned with flower petals and a spread of tarot cards. She's blissfully unaware of the red and white sign indicating 'No phones allowed' and films a wide sweeping video of the room, inclusive of all persons in it.

Our instructor, Wilma, is an older Australian woman with purple hair and feather earrings. She politely reminds everyone that no phones are allowed in the studio.

"Turn them off or switch them on airplane mode so we won't have any disturbances."

I glance at Running Girl, who clicks a button on the side of her phone before placing it face down in her lap.

Now there's an attachment.

I sit on my mat and glance around the room, smiling at the young woman next to me. A lady with dreadlocks waves to a latecomer hovering at the door, gesturing to the mat she's saved next to her. A heavily tattooed guy with a man bun approaches and she jumps up. They embrace tightly for several beats longer than necessary, suggesting a long overdue reunion or a public display of affection. I quickly look away.

"Alright everyone, let's get started."

Wilma guides the group through a seated meditation featuring whimsical sounds: she encircles a wand around a delicate crystal bowl, thrums a stick against a drum and shakes a cardboard tube filled with sand.

"Focus on your heart chakra, the whirling energy center in your chest. How does it feel? Is it glowing with love, or is there a blockage there?"

Wilma instructs us to think of someone we care for who might need some extra love right now. I think of my friend back home who recently lost her baby and send her a telepathic surge of love. Next, Wilma prompts the group to focus on someone we struggle to love; perhaps, even someone we need to forgive. I think of my megalomaniac ex who tried to control my diet, constantly pressuring me to eat meat after ten years of vegetarianism.

Suddenly, I become aware his harmful behavior was learned.

Hurt people, hurt people.

I remind myself resentment only hurts me, so I consciously relinquish any residual distaste I have for him. I take a note from the Tibetan monk at the meditation center in India and imagine my mind as a dumpster, visualizing my grudges as trash. I imagine tossing them into the bin and in doing so, forgiving.

Wilma guides us back to present awareness of the room.

"Wiggle your fingers and toes…slowly move your body and when you're ready to open your eyes, sit across from the person beside you."

I exchange an uncertain glance with my neighbor, offering her a small, contained smile.

"Prepare for an eye gazing meditation."

We shift our bodies to face one another and lock eyes. My partner looks to be in her early twenties with long, black hair piled into a thick ponytail. I look directly into her brown eyes, which have a sad quality to them.

"The eyes are the windows to the soul. Say hello, you are meeting your partner's essence."

At first, we smile and laugh to diffuse our shared discomfort, though there is nothing funny about this: it's awkward.

"It's totally natural to feel uncomfortable or emotional. It's not very often we allow ourselves to be seen like this."

A blonde lady near us begins to cry and Wilma steps towards her with a box of tissues.

"That's it, surrender to the moment," Wilma coos, placing a supportive hand on her shoulder. The woman continues to heave with ragged sobs.

I, on the other hand, am far from tears. Despite continuing to blink normally, my eyelids shutter with effort. I'm reminded of the wall sit exercise from Phys-ed class, where my thighs would burn and shake with exertion. My eyes desperately want to close. I don't think I've ever held eye contact with another human being for this long and it feels as if I might go cross-eyed. My partner's beautiful face even begins to contort like an abstract painting.

"If you need to take a break, close your eyes for a couple of seconds and then re-open them."

We both close our eyes for momentary reprieve and when we blink open, there's no more fake smiling or awkward laughing. I see a softening of her face, as if she's just exhaled a breath she was holding. The muscles around her eyes relax and just like that, her walls are down. I suppose mine must be too, because I feel something warm, light and familiar. It's as if I know her and feel love for her.

Her eyes well with tears and mine prickle. We smile and laugh, for real this time. It's as if we've just remembered something and giggle at the absurdity of how we could have forgotten it in the first place. Tears slide down her face now and I'm not sure she's crying from an emotional release, like the blonde lady who continues to weep. What we're experiencing isn't fear or overwhelm from the vulnerability of such intimacy, but a mutual marveling of it: the magic of truly seeing and being seen.

"Great job everyone. Take a few moments with your partner before coming to stand at the front of your mats."

The spell is broken. Whatever connection was shared between us is severed as quickly as it sparked. We exchange stiff and clunky small talk, swapping names and where we come from, but our words pale by comparison. She fidgets with her hands and glances down shyly and I see her walls of reserve go back up. Our moment of connectivity is gone.

"Your heart chakras are now open. Walk around the room and say hi to each other or give someone a hug."

I approach the blonde lady, whose puffy eyes continue to leak from her blotchy face. She lurches forward, latching onto me in a tight embrace. We part and I look into her eyes, offering her a genuine smile.

I take a slow lap of the room and come face-to-face with Running Girl. I'm pleasantly surprised when she approaches me with genuine kindness.

"You're so beautiful. I love your skirt! Can I hug you?"

She is young, innocent and energetic. I feel a surge of shame for being judgemental earlier, mistaking her enthusiasm for self-entitlement. I smile and take a step forward, wrapping my arms around her. I'm suddenly overwhelmed with emotion and don't know what to say, but maybe that's okay. I squeeze her for just a beat longer than necessary, before returning to my mat without a word.

Wilma ends the session by offering us an affirmation card from the deck splayed out in front of her mat. Meanwhile, my eye gazing partner immediately collects her tote bag from the side of the room and speeds off without saying goodbye. She may have been in a rush to leave, but I wager I wasn't alone in my awkwardness. The unexpected intimacy formed something like a 'vulnerability hangover', a sobering nakedness after relinquishing armor before a complete stranger.

The choice remains: put it back on and return to the safety of what's known or walk freely without its weight.

I relocate to a restaurant called 'Sun Sun Warung' on my way home. Inside a family compound, gamelan music plays in the background of a lush garden with purple and gold decor. I choose a low table near the altar, a statue adorned with a tall black umbrella with tassels, and sit cross-legged on a floor cushion.

My vegetarian nasi campur comes out—a platter with rice, grilled tempeh with peanut sauce, egg and coconut salad—and I graze while journaling. Writing is my favourite way to self-reflect, process and integrate life experiences; it's like a therapy session on paper.

I found the eye gazing meditation fascinating, and scribble down notes about my radically renewed perspective on eye contact. I'd never thought about it as particularly intimate, but after this experience my perception is changed. It's not that I can't or won't make eye contact; I just don't particularly like to. It's awkward and too intense at times, but now I wonder if it's the intimacy which feels this way: the vulnerability of 'being seen'.

Yet to be loved, is to be seen.

Behind my armor, I feel safe but inevitably, I'm unseen and therefore never truly known. We hide so much of ourselves away from the world, leaving words unsaid and feelings unprocessed. The eyes never lie though. They provide a reliable window, involuntarily expressing our joy or our deepest sorrows. Sometimes, it's just easier to look away.

I don't want to hide behind an iron shield anymore.

I glance around the garden and notice an advertisement for an inhouse gift shop. Canvas tote bags and t-shirts sport the slogan: "Nasi Campur is cheaper than therapy."

I put down my pen and take a cool sip of Jamu from the perspiring glass bottle, before spooning another bite of soft white rice.

It certainly is.

8

The Dragon House

I'm on the back of a Gojek, headed towards the neighborhood of Maas, a village in Ubud known for wood carving and sprawling rice paddies. I'm delivered to a parking lot and walk down a winding path to a crimson gate with a slithering brass Dragon: I've arrived at the 'Dragon House' for a weekend of dog sitting.

I knock and hear nothing.

I try the door and find it unlocked, slowly pushing inwards to reveal concrete steps leading down to the entrance of the home. At the base of the staircase, there's a large koi pond with stepping stones illuminated by dangling overhead lights, marking the entrance of a wrap-around corridor with high-ceilings.

Meandering down the steps, I feel like Alice in Wonderland as I notice a glass-enclosed lounge along the left of the koi pond. I turn left down the corridor, tiptoeing towards an open-air kitchen and vast sitting area with green and orange ornate furnishings and custom works of art.

"Hello?" I call out.

Karen told me to let myself in, but I'm suddenly shy having done so.

She pops her head around the corner and greets me.

"I'll be right down!"

I settle into a plush, lime green lounge chair and notice an infinity pool with a panoramic jungle view beyond the kitchen. The place is a dream, like something out of a luxury travel magazine.

I can see why they call it 'The Dragon House'. In addition to the brass dragon coiled around the front door, an intricate wood sculpture of a dragon sprawls along the pool. I would come to learn Anders and I share something in common: we were both born in the year of the Dragon. He resonates so much with the dragon archetype he designed his home to incorporate elements of 'dragon energy'. It's certainly an impressive space.

Karen takes me on the grand tour. Upstairs, the master bedroom is enclosed by glass with a custom circular bed in a shade of vibrant red and a striking boudoir portrait of a bare-chested Karen mounted on the wall. Back by the pool, a staircase leading to the lower level reveals a sauna and cold plunge tub, and three guest bedrooms. One, a funky David Bowie themed room, has a large window in the wall which peers directly into the deep end of the pool. The other two rooms have floor-to-ceiling doors opening into generous ensuite bathrooms with walk-in showers and spacious jungle decks.

The dogs, Bunny and Bella, are delightful creatures: like toddlers, they fight for my attention and affection. I wake in my canopy bed, thinking one of the many oversized pillows fell on top of my head, but no: it's a dog spooning my skull.

I reach up to stroke the soft curls and determine which beast is cuddling my head like a furry cap and can tell it's Bella by her tinier frame. They are easy dogs and don't require much exercise; just lots of love and companionship.

The sunrise peeks through the palm trees outside my floor to ceiling window, illuminating the foot of my bed like watercolor brushstrokes on a white canvas. I step out onto the deck facing the jungle, admiring sunbeams radiating through bamboo shoots and leafy trees.

I greet the girls with good morning head scratches, and we retrace our way up the concrete steps beyond the crimson door, where they use the leafy garden as a bathroom.

As the day unfolds, it becomes apparent Bunny is not okay. She lays, panting and listless with a blank stare, and her rotund belly is hot. Karen is immediately responsive and has an emergency vet come to the house.

A kind Balinese man briefly examines Bunny before deciding he needs to take her to his clinic in Denpasar for further testing. He attempts to lift her and she resists, clearly terrified of a stranger taking her, so I make a split decision to ride with her on my lap in the back of his van.

At the clinic, they hook her up to an IV and run a few tests before deciding to keep her overnight for observation. She's placed alone in a little penned off area, confused and scared, and I cry leaving her there.

All the while, I've continued to text American Matt, on and off, since our failed yoga date. In the time that's passed, we've met twice for food or coffee, but our communication is sparse and lack-luster. He often mentions how busy he is and even 'double tapped' one of my messages, leaving a heart emoji reaction rather than an actual response. I don't feel a romantic resonance with him, but I keep in touch nonetheless because he's one of the few people I know in town.

I relay to him via text, the gorgeous house I'm looking after and the unfortunate series of events with Bunny. He suggests stopping by for a visit to bring me takeaway. I had no time to stock my fridge with groceries under the circumstances, so this sounds quite pleasant after such a stressful ordeal.

Gratefully, I'm able to bring Bunny home the next day but by the time we return to the Dragon House, it's dark. I'm exhausted, starving and somewhat regretting my plans, yet I don't cancel on Matt. Wouldn't it be inconsiderate so last minute? I mean, what if he was waiting around all evening for me?

Matt arrives with combed hair and ample cologne but no takeaway. I'm stunned into submission, too awkward to inquire about the takeaway (or lack thereof).

Maybe I misunderstood?

I don't even have a beverage to offer him, as I assumed he was bringing the meal, so we sit with cups of water, and I attempt to have a functional conversation while running on empty.

We move into the air-conditioned lounge and sit on the couch where the dogs are snoozing. He slowly sides closer and I'm acutely aware of the sudden repositioning of his body next to mine. It makes me profusely uncomfortable and on-edge.

I shift away, reasserting my personal space. He slides in again. I pick up Bella, the smaller poodle, and place her in my lap, anxiously stroking her soft curls.

Matt becomes visibly annoyed, outwardly asking me in frustration what we are doing, if we aren't doing 'that'.

"I'm attracted to you, but I haven't been able to read you, like I want to kiss you but every time I move towards you, you lean away or place a dog between us. I'm just not sure what we are doing here."

I don't know what we're doing either. Our sporadic communication, with him repeatedly telling me how busy he was, hadn't exactly sparked my affections for him. I only entertained this meeting because I interpreted his offer of dinner as a sweet gesture to remedy my stressful day, expecting a shared meal, not an ultimatum.

"Have you always been this aloof?"

He's looking directly into my eyes now.

I pause, digesting what he's just said.

He quickly adds, "Well some people are, so I was just wondering if you were always this way."

Somehow, I didn't pick up on the social cues[9] of what him coming to my place at night symbolized until this very moment and am blindsided by the realization of why he really came here, empty handed no less.

---

[9]In hindsight, I recognize my naivety in this situation. When he proposed a night in with take out, I took it as a literal statement that he would be bringing me take away food. Frankly, the prospect was a comfort after the stressful day I had with a sick animal. I wish I could say this was an isolated incident, but I have a propensity for misunderstanding social cues in dating (such as being completely shocked by unwanted advances during a 'netflix and chill' date because I expected to simply eat popcorn and watch a movie).

My heart beats faster and my tummy churns with hurt, perhaps even betrayal. Casting my gaze downwards, in efforts to steel my resolve not to cry, I steady my voice.

"It just takes me a while to get comfortable with someone."

"I'm open to helping you explore that, if you want to. I'm not trying to pressure you though," he offers, without breaking eye contact.

My skin crawls.

I wish I could say I called him out, told him off, and promptly asked him to leave, but the thing is, my survival mode is not always fight or flight: sometimes it's 'freeze'. It can feel safer to coast along through an uncomfortable encounter, appeasing the other person's ego to not trigger it into escalation, a far more dangerous scenario with a man clearly motivated by one thing.

So no, I don't tell him to fuck off.

I feign a nonchalant neutral acceptance that 'I am, the way I am' and tell him I'd rather take things slow.

"It must be hard for people to wait around that long."

After only meeting three times, I'm flabbergasted by Matt's entitlement to my body in exchange for his time (which he clearly feels he's invested too much of with no reward). When I didn't respond to his advances in the way he wanted me to, he projected a deficit onto me, an apparent intimacy issue he could help me overcome.

I saw straight through the charade.

I desperately want him to leave, but torrential rains have started. We wait for the weather to die down in an awkwardness so thick I might simply pass away from mortification, but even still, I want him to get home safely.

After Matt leaves, I'm furious, but mostly at myself for not saying what I wanted to in the moment. Instead, I'm haunted for hours as I lay awake, rehearsing what I should have said and how I should have reacted. It's now a one-sided conversation because I know with resounding certainty, I will never speak to him again.

Silence can sometimes communciate far more than words.

9

Take Me to Church

Still upset by my interaction with creepy Matt, I decide to work off my rage in a healthy way: power yoga. There's a class at Yoga Barn the following day with live musicians to accompany fast-paced sequences, and I resolve to go.

Karen left me her car and I'm nervous at the mere thought of driving in Ubud on the opposite side of the road I'm used to. When I sit behind the wheel of the automatic transmission though, my muscle memory kicks in.

I cautiously edge the four-door sedan out of the parking lot and onto a narrow road surrounded by vast rice fields and palm trees. The car hugs a tight curve to reveal an upcoming road—a major road. I need to turn against two lanes of oncoming vehicles and honking scooters. It's apparent this will require patience and radical confidence in my driving capabilities as I wait for a lull in traffic. I see my opportunity and without hesitation, crank the steering wheel right, whizzing across the road to head North. Easing the car up the Yoga Barn's steep driveway, I park and exhale with relief. I celebrate this tiny moment of success: I've conquered my first drive in Bali!

Meandering through the bustling property, I climb the same spiral stairs to the loft studio. It's packed with nearly one hundred bodies atop yoga mats pressed side-by-side like sardines in a can. Some folks are quietly sitting in meditation, while others whisper affectionate greeting to friends.

I awkwardly hover at the door, scanning the room for an empty space. One kind soul gestures to me, pointing to a spot in front of her which would narrowly fit a yoga mat if the woman at the end of the row shifted slightly. I crouch down on my haunches and look at her, smiling expectantly.

"Hi," I whisper, "Is it ok if I go here?"

She looks at me flatly. After an uncomfortable pause, she says in a thick French accent, "No, I don't think there is space, it won't work."

"Where else am I supposed to go?"

She shrugs as if it isn't her problem.

I glance around the room and notice a similar sized space one row away and turn without another word. Claiming the spot without asking this time, I smile at both ladies on either side, who to my relief return the gesture.

It gives me inordinate pleasure when the yoga teacher asks us to make space for late comers, reminding us to be generous to our fellow yogis. I glance back and a topless man in tiny shorts has claimed the spot beside the French lady. He appears to be quite sweaty, probably on account of his thick body hair resembling a coating of fur. I resist the urge to smirk, because that wouldn't be very yogic, would it?

As we wait for class to begin, our teacher introduces himself to the group as Chad. He confidently struts around the room, approaching people in embraces as if they are long lost friends, followed by, "What's your name brother?" and "Welcome sister."

I avoid eye contact, so he won't approach me, casting my gaze downward, which unfortunately gives me privy to the hairy knuckles of his dirty feet as he steps directly onto my mat.

Bilbo Baggins has entered the chat.

He is blissfully unaware I will spend the next hour trying to avoid his invisible footprint. Otherwise, my face could touch it, which would be like him pressing the sole of his foot to my cheek like an oversized, smelly telephone.

The pure mental imagery sends a visceral wave of ick through my body, like tiny bugs crawling under my skin. Involuntarily, I clench my fists and hold my breath. The irony of yoga class causing more anxiety than it alleviates, is not lost on me, but here we are, and class is about to begin.

"Welcome to Yoga Barn," Chad booms.

"It doesn't get more yoga than this," he says as he glides to the front of the shala like a preacher climbing the stairs to his pulpit.

I mean, maybe in India.

Chad takes an audible deep breath and noisily releases wet sounding air into the head-strapped microphone hugging the curve of his skull.

"Living versus existing," he croons, allowing those three simple words to suspend in a dramatic pause.

"Existing is what we do when we aren't present in the moment but living—truly living—means slowing down enough to notice the transformation as it's happening."

He has a point.

Since coming to Bali, my life has slowed down to an uncomfortable snail-paced crawl. I'm not used to having a schedule not packed to the brim, and it's become evident I don't know how to relax.

This is meant to be a time of rest, yet I subconsciously clung to the idea my value is intricately intertwined with my ability to be productive. I feet an inherent need to 'make the most' of my time away from work, prescribing myself a rigid routine filled with meditation, yoga, journaling, and an array of holistic treatments. I'm a chronic overachiever, ambitiously pursuing spirituality and wellness as if they're accolades to add to my list of accomplishments.

I flung myself back into dating as a desperate attempt for connection but am not achieving the caliber of connection I seek, making me feel worse as a result.

Am I just distracting myself, from myself?

The truth is, if I actually surrender to the void of stillness, I'll be forced to face the root cause of my behavior over the past year. I can relate to Chad's notion of 'witnessing the transformation': the fact I'm even having these introspective revelations means it's begun for me here in Ubud.

"The frequency of truth is all we have."

He allows the sentence to hang momentarily in silence. I'm not sure what exactly this means, but I like his philosophical musings. However, I strongly question his guarantee this moment and this class (his class) is going to transform us, as if he alone can offer yogic emancipation from mere existence to transcendence.

To me, existence is perhaps all we have: a changing, impermanent state of being we humans don't fully understand. Perhaps my relentless pursuit of my life's purpose is futile when I've yet to grasp the purpose of life itself.

Since childhood, I had an acute awareness of my own mortality, prompting me to question life and the Christian religion I was raised in. I asked existential questions no one could definitively answer.

"What happens after we die? Is heaven an actual place? Why can't we remember being born? Why do we dream? Why do bad things happen to good people? Why do some people die so young? If we're all just going to die anyway, then what's the point?"

My questions made people uncomfortable and sometimes even angry, so I learned it was safer to be quiet, earning me the label of a shy and timid child. My mind was anything but quiet though.

Dressed in my Sunday best, I'd sit in Church silent but viscerally disturbed by another church-goer's inconspicuous removal of sore feet from stiff shoes, wiggling life back into their stocking-clad toes beneath the bible-lined pew. The resulting repugnant aroma could have knocked an angel clear from the sky, a sin requiring repentance in my opinion, but I digress.

It was around this time I discovered I could disconnect from my body, existing almost entirely in my head. As a teen, my over-active mind began to fester into repressed, raging anxiety I eventually tampered with alcohol throughout my adulthood. It's only now, on my self-imposed wellness regime in Bali, that I quit alcohol entirely, my longest stretch without a drink in over 15 years.

Maybe the 'frequency of truth' Chad speaks of is just humility: admitting we don't know everything and granting ourselves grace as we navigate those spaces of unknown.

The musicians begin to play a harmonium, guitar and flute, while the singer gently harmonizes with lyrics. Chad periodically warbles into his microphone in the absent-minded way one randomly sings along to a song on the radio, but his voice is less than melodic, eclipsing the beautiful singer. I become distracted by imagining her inner monologue as his amplified voice belts over hers.

Towards the end of the class, Chad cues us to come into mountain pose, a standing posture with our eyes closed. After a few breaths, he guides us into 'intuitive movement of the spine', which quickly escalates into a moment of unbridled ecstatic dance[10]. The musicians rise to the occasion, picking up a rapid instrumental pace.

"Come closer everyone, towards the center!" Chad hollers.

He begins to enthusiastically jump up and down, hands outstretched wide to the heavens like a worshiper praising his God. He jumps so high, he nearly levitates right off the floor, reminding me of a pogo stick (though I'm sure he'd prefer the metaphor of Jesus himself hovering over water).

---

[10]Ecstatic dance is an intuitive and improvised style of dancing that encourages people to move freely to music on their own or with others. In Bali, ecstatic dance is offered as an event at many yoga establishments and is exceedingly popular among the tourists and expats in Ubud.

He was beginning to remind me of my megalomaniac ex with a stubborn superiority complex. The same one who frequently became enraged when I'd reject his unsolicited nutrition advice, such as the benefits of a 'Cave Man' diet. I finally broken things off when he compared himself to 'He who has Risen', with noble intentions of trying to 'save me from myself' (and evidently, also from vegetarianism). It was alarming to say the least and took the meaning of 'What Would Jesus Do' to a whole new extreme.

We continue to bounce along to a manic rhythm, some surrendering to the moment with hands raised to the sky, while others more visibly uncomfortable, glance around while feigning half-hearted bounces on their heels. I close my eyes and allow my body to move freely to the music. My hair coiled in a top-knot, bobs and loosens with each jump, until tendrils of unruly hair fall down my face, sticking in free-flowing sweat.

The group returns to silent stillness, standing and eventually laying, with one hand over our racing hearts and the other resting on our bellies, allowing our breath to slow. To end the class, Chad encourages us to sit cross-legged around the band, creating a half-moon arc of bodies. The musicians start a slow, gentle song: Lokah Samastah Sukhino

Bhavantu. I later learn this is a beautiful Sanskrit prayer, roughly translating to: "may all beings everywhere be happy and free, and may the thoughts, words and actions of my own life contribute in some way to the happiness and freedom of all."

"Everybody now!" yells Chad.

My voice is barely audible, clumsily whispering unfamiliar words I don't quite know, nor understand, while more confident and harmonious voices buoyantly lift from the group.

Chad concludes our session by chanting, "shiva om, shiva om, shiva om," before reminding us to scan the QR code by the door to follow him on Instagram.

I worked up an appetite with all that hopping around and decide to return to Sayuri Healing Foods, the same vegan restaurant I dined with Karen, Anders and Xavier. I recall its location being just down the street, so I hop in Karen's sedan and slowly inch down the sharp laneway, hanging a left onto Sukma Kesuma road.

Although the traffic has significantly died off by now, the street is poorly illuminated and I'm nervous driving in the dark. I reach a three-way stop and follow a motorbike straight towards Sayuri, unaware I've just entered a one-way street and am now driving in the wrong direction.

Even if I'd seen the street sign prohibiting cars from entering, I wouldn't have been able to read the text printed in Bahasa. To add to the confusion, motorbikes are still allowed to travel in both directions, so I assumed the street is bi-directional when the scooter in front of me continued straight.

I quickly realize my mistake when a van barrels towards me, abruptly breaking and flashing its high beams. To my horror, there is no space to turn around or get out of the way. The narrow road is consumed by parked cars and motorbikes along the median.

Shit.

Flustered now, I check there are no pedestrians before hopping the curb onto the sidewalk to let the oncoming van (and long line of bikes behind it) pass by.

My heart is beating wildly as I wait for a break in traffic to turn the car around on the narrow road. It would be tricky and not too unlike the scene I'm now mentally conjuring from the film Austin Powers, when the 'International Man of Mystery' manages to tightly wedge a golf cart between two walls.

I edge the car off the curb and lurch forward, pulling into a short laneway before slowly reversing in the opposite direction—when I hear a sharp, animalistic scream. The road is dark and it's difficult to appreciate what is making the noise. I'm now in a heightened state of anxiety, profusely worrying I've hit an animal.

I gently tuck the car in behind another parked vehicle and switch off the engine, listening. It sounds like a monkey, but surely, they wouldn't wander so far from Ubud's monkey forest? It could be possible I guess, I'm not exactly an expert on the migration patterns of the common primate.

I clamber out of the driver's seat and breathe a sigh of relief: the monkey-like screams are emanating from a man. He's 'oooo-ooo-ing' and 'ahhh-ahhh-ingg' to alert attention to the basket of goods on top of his head. I give him credit for his marketing strategy, because he certainly caught my attention. I would later find out the Ape man is a relic among several Ubudian neighborhoods, known for his monkey mouth and the street food he peddles.

I walk the rest of the way to the restaurant, shaking my head and chuckling.

While I may attract chaos, at least I always have a story to tell.

10

A Healing

Karen and Anders return from their weekend away, raving about a spirit festival they participated in down in Uluwatu. They're exceedingly grateful I'd taken such good care of Bunny during her illness and Karen wraps me in her arms.

"I was so relieved when you offered to go to the clinic with Buns, she must have been so frightened, we just can't thank you enough."

She offers to drive me home, but first, we ride around for a while in search of street dogs, pulling over to offer them food. Karen has brought a large container of fatty, grizzled meat leftover from a roast chicken. We spot two scruffy dogs lazing in the shade and she dishes out a handful of meat to each, cautiously placing it on the ground from a safe distance for them to approach. She reminds me not to feed from the hand, as some street dogs can become aggressive around food.

I can tell she's done this before. Karen tells me Bali has a street dog problem and while there are countless vet clinics, rescue centers and sanctuaries doing good work, they operate at maximum capacity with buckling resources. There's a resulting push for sterilization, with annual rounds to fix the street dogs, yet it's still common to find litters of pups dumped in rice fields or outside an unsuspecting expat's villa.

Karen used to run a puppy cafe on the beach, where stray dogs found sanctuary and patrons could come for a cuppa and a cuddle. Sadly, the pandemic and frequent poisonings of dogs on the beach forced her to shut down, requiring an immediate relocation of all beach dogs for their safety. Rat poison is a common method of dealing with street dogs, though no one is certain who is behind the cullings.

Back at home in my jungle flat, I lay lifeless on my bed with a strong desire for silence and solitude. It was a treat to stay in such a luxurious space for a few nights, but the stress of tending to a sick animal, the interaction with creepy Matt, and the mental energy spent driving, have left me drained. The familiar signs of anxiety and overwhelm rise like a dense fog over my body. I pushed myself too hard yet again.

Almost immediately, I fall into a deep sleep.

I wake up on my back in darkness with the sensation I'm not alone, as if someone is watching me. I sense the presence of something in the corner of the room, and it inches towards the bed. I try to move but I'm frozen.

I drift back into a deep sleep.

Again, I startle awake completely paralyzed on my back. This time I sense 'something' perched on my chest. I hear an animalistic sniffing and feel a flow of air above my face, as if something is inhaling my scent or my lifeforce, like a rogue dementor in Harry Potter.

I scream, but no sound escapes my mouth.

It's far from my first run-in with sleep paralysis. I experienced the phenomenon on and off for a decade, but it's my first time having an episode while living in a place where cultural and religious beliefs in spirits are prevalent.

According to Balinese cosmology, the universe contains two properties: *sekala*, which can be perceived with the five senses, and *niskala*, which cannot be perceived by the senses. The world is a mix of sekala and niskala: comprised of the heavens, the middle space where humans live, and the underworld.

The preservation of balance and harmony between these spaces and properties is of vital importance, necessitating the daily ritual of canang sari, the ubiquitous daily offering placed on altars and at doorways to ward off angry spirits.

In fact, spiritual harmony is the first consideration prior to building a new home. A religious land ceremony is mandatory prior to construction, to ensure the spirits residing there are successfully relocated. Balinese homes are then intentionally constructed with spiritual protection in mind, typically including six-foot walls around the compound and a temple. Daily offerings left at the primary entrance are never missed. I've even seen them adorning car dashboard and scooters, protecting the driver and passengers.

I scour the internet for potential leads, trying to find a Balinese interpretation of sleep paralysis and stumble upon an article describing 'Tonya', a spirit residing in rivers, which can become angry when displaced. I immediately think of my jungle flat[11] overlooking a ravine, void of any protective walls, altar or offerings. Were the spirits of the river below disturbed by the flat and by extension, my presence? Or were my episodes of sleep paralysis merely stress induced nightmares?

---

[11] A Balinese friend later told me this area of Penestanan is near a local cemetery with a lot of spirits. According to their beliefs, I was most likely visited by an 'orb', but my aura was strong enough to fight it off.

In North America, I would be diagnosed with a mental disorder, but in Bali the explanation is starkly different: I'm being visited by something otherworldly. When a person experiences a conflict or crisis, such as reoccurring nightmares, the Balinese assume there's an imbalance of the physical and spiritual planes, requiring a purification ritual to restore harmony.

I decide to seek a Balinese healer.

Wayan Nuriasih is the female healer featured in the book and film 'Eat Pray Love'. It was never my intention to visit her out of fandom, or to follow in the author's footsteps, but rather I stumbled on her business by chance.

I joined a Facebook Group for Women in Bali to connect with other solo females and make new friends. The page is also commonly used as a 'buy and sell', where girls leaving the island advertise moving sales. I'd come to Bali straight from an Irish Winter and didn't have a large summer wardrobe, so I was drawn to several dresses listed by a girl named Josie. She suggested I come over to try them on, so I ordered a Gojek to her villa, just north of the center of town towards the popular Tegalalang rice paddies.

After buying a few flowy sundresses and belly tops, I waited outside for a Gojek to bring me home and noticed a green sign across the road with bold capital letters: 'EAT PRAY LOVE'. I recognized Wayan's name and snapped a photo of the sign advertising energy healing sessions.

Now, I pull up the photo in my phone and re-read the details on the sign. I'm not clear what an energy healing session involves, but I'm in my healing era and open to trying anything that might help me.

I order a Gojek and arrive outside the compound where I first saw the road-side sign. A Brazilian couple are waiting outside the gated entrance, and I hover near them. A younger Canadian woman joins after me, forming a short queue which reaches the road, a bustling street with motorbikes whizzing back and forth.

Wayan opens the gate and stands, blocking the entrance. She wears a crisp white blouse and lilac skirt, and her dark hair is twisted into a claw-clip. She holds a clipboard and resembles a stern school teacher, silently examining us through rectangular spectacles. I wait for her to invite us in, but she remains stationary at the gate, handing us an intake form. We are instructed to write our full name, place of birth and birthday, including the day of the week.[12]

Wayan has each of us step up to the gate for a brief introduction, before shooing us away and motioning to the

---

[12]I was born on a Tuesday. According to the calendar system used by Balinese Hindus, people born on Tuesdays are quiet, charismatic, stubborn and very smart but can at times be irrational or suspicious…hmm, sounds about right.

next. The gated entrance we crowd around is only a few steps from the road and it's difficult to hear her voice over the traffic. A wave of disappointment rolls through me. I anticipated a more private setting than this, perhaps even an opportunity to sit down with Wayan. She's speaking to one of my companions, when she suddenly stops and looks directly at me:

"I do not allow people into my property without a cleansing ritual, it brings bad spirits, bad things happen before we do this."

I'm startled, as though she's just read my mind. What if she senses the reason for my visit and the cause of my sleep paralysis, and this is why we've been blocked at the gate?

I shake off the thought, but am humbled into submission. I silently step forward when it's my turn to approach her.

Wayan has me outstretch my hands, palms facing up, and examines them through her reading glasses.

"Pain in stomach, yes, pain in stomach, digestion not so good," she says while scribbling notes on my form.

"You have pineapple, next day mango, next day spicey, next day coffee, not all at same time or too much acid," she instructs.

She pauses to check the progress of the Canadian girl behind me, who was instructed to apply a gray paste to her stomach. Wayan uses her pen to demonstrate, poking her own belly.

"You put inside belly button. See, you feel better already!"

Wayan returns to my outstretched hands as if gazing into a looking glass and continues diagnosing me.

"Neck and shoulder pain too." She nonchalantly ticks a box on her form.

Using the tip of her pen, she flips my hands over, examining the tops, and reaches for an offering from a nearby basket. She holds it high over her head and chants a prayer for me in Bahasa.

Returning her gaze to mine, she tells me, "Three generations from your papa, they are healer people." Nodding in affirmation, she confirms, "You can learn healing."

There is a generous pause before she asks, "What do you do?"

Momentarily stunned, my thoughts fail to properly link with my speech. I blurt out, "Medical."

"Huh?" she asks.

How can I possibly explain to her I'm a researcher by background, with a prior career in health care and a failed yoga business, but I'm currently unemployed on a career break; and oh yah, I'm also a travel blogger.

I realize what I've said didn't make sense, but it comes out again:

"Medical."

"I'm a medical researcher," I tell her.

The Brazilian man behind me has been listening with interest. "Ahhh, general practitioner," he says in a thick Portuguese accent, nodding in approval.

"Researcher," I correct him, now speaking more to him than to Wayan, and he steps in as a makeshift interpreter, saying loudly over my head: "Investigation. She makes research."

Wayan nods in acknowledgement and looks me square in the eyes.

"You must learn healing. This is your part-time job now. You must learn something. If you don't, it will confuse your mind, cause problem, long time pain in neck."

Unsure of how to react, I silently nod, as she leans forward and pulls down my lower eyelids to examine the whites of my eyes. "Low blood pressure," she nods, adding another tick to my form.

She pinches one of my fingertips.

"You're smart, not a stupid person," she adds, vigorously shaking her head. "Not stupid, very smart."

Her stern demeanor finally breaks, and she giggles.

"Your mind is like this," she says, drawing a straight line which forks into two directions. She rotates one of her hands back and forth for extra effect, as if opening and closing a jar.

Wayan prescribes me rice porridge and star gooseberry leaf, though I'm unclear for what, and offers me a small, clear bag of green goo to put on my face.

"Now," she instructs.

I step aside and begin to apply the paste to my face like a mud mask. I look like Shrek and people on motorbikes gawk as they drive by.

I watch on with intrigue as the Brazilian man is instructed to get down on his knees for an onion-water cleansing. She sprinkles it over his head like a root vegetable baptism, while he pats the holy water over his face and head.

"My eyes, it burns," he exclaims, blindly stumbling to the outdoor wash basin to rinse his face.

I follow him to wash the green crust off my skin and return to the gate to hear final remarks from Wayan.

"You must calm the mind, you learn meditation, then you will be healing."

The experience was admittedly not what I expected, but Wayan was extremely accurate. I do have neck pain and digestive issues, I've experienced fainting spells from low blood pressure, and I certainly struggle to calm my mind.

Yet, I accept her prophecy with hesitancy. For all I know, she could tell every visitor they're meant to be a healer, playing into the egos of tourists on a spiritual quest.

While I recognize this is cynical, it's a valid consideration in the wake of the vast success of 'Eat Pray Love' and its resulting impact on Bali, and in particular Ubud. It's no coincidence Ubud has become a hub for new-age spirituality to the extent that the bulk of its 'spiritual experiences' are not recognizably Balinese.

Hordes of female tourists descend upon Ubud on their own soul-searching journeys, eager to find themselves by way of the heart opening cacao ceremonies, self-love meditations or womb circles marketed to them. It requires discernment to determine which offerings are steeped in centuries of Balinese tradition and ancestral knowledge, from those appropriated and packaged to meet tourist demand.

Strikingly, many classes and workshops I tried were facilitated by white instructors in ways which feel reminiscent of North America. Practices I understand to be 'closed', or only led by shamans or healers of Indigenous origin, are sprinkled into events and workshops like decoration. Advertisements are posted around town for 'plant medicine journeys' with Ayahuasca and even kambo ceremonies, involving the application of poisonous frog secretions to the skin.

Drugs are highly illegal in Indonesia and it's unclear where plant and frog medicine fall into the legislation, nor how regulated these substances are. Laws aside, it's striking to find South American healing rituals facilitated by white foreigners on a tiny island in Southeast Asia.

Components of Hinduism and Buddhism are integrated into in nearly every yoga class or spiritual event but rarely unpacked and taught. Rather, attendees collectively chant ancient Sanskrit text without understanding what it translates to, or pray to Gods and deities, like Lord Ganesha the elephant God, without knowledge of whom they worship. Something about it makes me uncomfortable.

While I'm acutely aware I perfectly fall into the trope of the woman who comes to Bali to heal, I think the conversation is bigger than a stereotype of privileged, dissatisfied and unfulfilled women on missions to find themselves.

Is it privileged to go soul-searching in Bali?

Absolutely.

The ability to take time off work, to afford the costs of travel and to have citizenship which grants global mobility are massive privileges.

Practicing mindfulness doesn't require a trip to Bali, but it's undoubtedly a destination rooted in rich culture, religion and unique spiritual beliefs. The dialogue needs to expand beyond those who come here as spiritual tourists, to ethical and sustainable tourism which doesn't appropriate cultural and religious practices, but rather connects spiritual seekers to Balinese teachers.

It remains unclear if Wayan's prophecy is genuine or part of a tourist trap, but simultaneously, I know I won't find what I'm looking for in the new-age spiritual community of Ubud.

11

A New Homebase

I am six years old, sitting in a field of grass at a baseball game. My Grandmother sits beside me and animatedly cheers for the team with a cow bell. Too young to be embarrassed by such behavior, I'm infatuated with the cow bell, and she lets me ring it too.

We're watching my Dad's recreational league play, but I'm bored by the game. I pick shards of grass from the ground and notice ants crawling onto our blanket spread across the field. I squash them one by one under my tiny thumb.

"Stop that!"

I jump.

I hadn't realized she was watching me.

"Why? They're just ants."

"How would you like it if someone bigger than you, picked on you just because you're little?"

I understand her point and look down with a guilty conscience.

It's a lesson I've never forgotten.

I've spent most of my life preoccupied with animals, pet sitting my way around the world and adopting vegetarianism in my twenties. It's been ten years since I've eaten any kind of meat, but even still, I struggle to hold compassion for Earthly creatures of the creepy, crawly kind.

I've become completely immune to spiders and geckos common in Bali, even going as far as naming them to make them less threatening in my mind. I know for a fact, there are geckos in this rental: the small ones leave little turds on every surface and the big one—a tokay gecko I've named Norman—loudly chirps like a bird.

Norm startles me each evening when I switch on the kitchen light and find him lurking. To be fair, I must startle him too, because he quickly slithers away across the ceiling and around the brick wall. Norm hunts mosquitos though and I love him for that—get your lunch king!

I digress, I'm still disturbed by Bali's arthropods. The other day, I found a creepy millipede the width of thick rope casually scuttling though my bathroom. I was horrified.

Yet its only crime is being small.

It's not like I could kill the thing even if I wanted to. The sheer thought of the crunch it would make under a shoe and any slime it might squirt is far worse than the millipede's unwanted presence. With resignation, I collected a hefty leaf from the garden for the little gaffer to climb on board before relocating him down to the grassy area by the jungle deck.

Nonetheless, I'm paranoid that one day, when unsuspecting and vulnerable in meditation, he might find me. I'm uncertain if this will be for a warm reunion or to enact revenge, but even the remote possibility of hundreds of tiny legs crawling over my foot, or worse, up my back, sends chills down my spine.

Wait, can they even crawl vertically?

I mentally calculate the probability that a millipede might crawl on me during meditation, before realizing that I'm supposed to be meditating right now. I'm sitting cross-legged on the jungle deck, eyes closed and evidently, deeply distracted by my incessant thoughts.

Inhale. One. Exhale. One.

Inhale. Two. Exhale. Two.

Inhale. Three. Exhale Three.

Inhale. Four. Exhale Four.

Inhale. Five. Exhale Five.

Can millipedes swim?

My jungle flat rental is approaching its end date and I'm internally debating what to do. I'm content in the Penestanan Kaja village, surrounded by quiet rice paddies, but also desire to see other parts of the island.

"I would also like a writing desk," I say out loud to myself.

I'd resorted to sitting cross-legged on my jungle deck, hunched over my journal like a Gremlin. My resulting hunchback was keeping my masseuse at Starchild Spa busy.

Quite serendipitously, I meet a German lady staying in the flat closest to mine and it comes up in conversation that I recently finished a weekend house sit to watch two dogs. She tells me she knows a Spanish woman who does long-term house sitting and insists I must connect with her. She scribbles her number on a slip of paper and tells me to text her so she can introduce us.

It turns out that Flora, the Spanish woman, is in a bind. She's currently dog sitting, and the dog owner is unable to return on the originally planned date, meaning she cannot start her next house sit. She asks if by chance I would be interested, describing a lovely two-bedroom home with three cats in Ubud, and I impulsively say yes.

Flora connects me to Ana, and we arrange a time for me

to stop by to meet her and the cats. She sends a pin-drop to the location, and I'm flabbergasted: it's the neighboring property directly across from my jungle flat!

I walk over to meet Ana, who is a sweet and vibrant marine biologist with wavy brown hair and bright eyes. She greets me with a hug and leads me down several stone steps to an open-air kitchen. We sit at a rectangular table with glasses of coconut water, and she tells me about herself. She's a program manager spearheading a coral reef preservation project out of Makassar, a port city on Indonesia's Eastern Island of Sulawesi. She adores Bali and keeps a homebase here so she can return on long weekends, holidays and periods when she's able to work remotely. Plus, she's adopted three cats that permanently live here.

Neo is a large, white furball with striking blue eyes, who curiously greets me by jumping on the table and rubbing his face into my outstretched hand. I'm not surprised, when in true cat form, he affectionately nips my thumb.

"This is his signature move when he's begging for treats," Ana says, gesturing to the fridge where she stows them for safe keeping. She submits and pulls out the packet, which attracts Neva, a much smaller cat with green eyes and a tortoise shell coat.

Echo is the most timid of the three, and we find her asleep on Ana's bed. She says hello with a high-pitched mew that quickly turns into a purr, before suckling her back paw like a baby with a bottle. I must have passed the cat test or Ana is desperate for a house sitter, because she offers me her spare room on an indefinite basis.

"You'd have plenty of time to travel to other parts of the island if you want to. We can coordinate the dates when I'm back so you can go off and explore."

I ask about Wi-Fi, and she leads me back outside, where I notice for the first time, a detached and enclosed room just past the kitchen: it's a home office with a writing desk!

"Of course everything is included, in exchange for you loving my cats while I'm gone."

I'm being gifted everything I asked for.

"Do you drive a bike?" she asks. "You're welcome to use my scooter too."

I exclusively used Gojek motorcycle taxis for the last few months; perhaps it's time for me to learn how to drive a scooter.

The timing works perfectly. I'll check out of my jungle flat and have a week to travel before starting the house sit. I decide to visit the popular Canggu neighborhood to see what the fuss is all about.

12

The Treehouse

I leave my luggage with Ana and check into a treehouse for the night, a short taxi ride away from the hustle and bustle of Canggu.

I shimmy up a narrow plank, like something from an obstacle course, and reach an open-air kitchen and lounge. There is a door leading to an enclosed bedroom and an outdoor bathroom, and a rickety ladder that pokes through a square porthole to an upper level.

The upstairs has a thatched roof and zero walls, revealing a panoramic view of rice fields to the front and a ravine surrounded by a jungle at the back. There's a second bed enveloped by a mosquito net, offering a more rustic sleeping experience. A thrill of excitement courses through me and I sink into a cushy bean bag chair beside a coffee table to take it all in.

I clamber back down the ladder to unpack items into the mini fridge and begin to prepare a simple dinner, turning on music while I cook. Dancing freely, I wildly undulate my limbs in an unbridled moment of joy—until I hear a shifting noise.

I turn off the music and pause, listening.

I realize I can smell cigarette smoke, which isn't entirely unusual in Bali, except this tree house is remote: there's no one else around.

I glance down and through a crack between the floorboards, I see a pair of men's feet. There is a man standing underneath the treehouse.

Thinking it might be the Airbnb host who checked me in earlier, I take a step towards the edge of the kitchen. Perhaps he's returned to do a quick maintenance task under there? Though I'd be surprised; hosts aren't supposed to stop by unannounced like this. The edge of the kitchen has a thin rope strung horizontally to act as a guard rail from the steep drop to the ground and I attempt to look down without falling.

There is a strange man under the treehouse smoking a cigarette.

Surely, he knows the space is occupied. He'd have heard my music, and probably saw my dance moves on account of the lack of walls. So why was he here, sneaking around under there?

A nervousness begins to churn in my belly: a warning sign of danger.

I gather my most serious face and aggressive tone, looking down sternly at him.

"Can I help you? Why are you here?"

He stares blankly, in the kind of expression that suggests he does not understand, when a language barrier renders words meaningless to the listener. He holds up a fishing rod, and silently walks away towards the river, where I realize there are two other men standing, looking up at me.

From the riverbank, there's a clear view directly into the outdoor shower. I'm not suggesting they are peeping Toms. In fact, they continue downriver, further out of sight, but the interaction leaves me vulnerable and nervous. Now there are three men that know I'm staying here alone and for obvious reasons, it's not the most secure space: anyone can walk across the plank to get up here.

I message the host to relay the interaction, and he promptly comes over to check on me, posting a private property sign. At the same time, I know the locals have a right to fish the river and don't expect them to stop on my account.

It's just the sad reality of being a woman alone: *my solitude makes me more vulnerable.*

Unfortunately, no one can automatically discern by first glance whether a stranger has good or bad intentions. For my own safety, I must look out for myself and assume that someone who enters my space uninvited and unannounced is a threat. As darkness quickly approaches, I consider the worst-case scenario.

What if the men return?

The bedroom adjacent to the kitchen has a locking door, but it's excruciatingly stuffy and riddled with biting ants. The upstairs bed with mosquito netting is a far superior choice due to a generous cross breeze, but the hinged flap closing off the porthole entrance doesn't lock.

I decide to sleep upstairs, with a booby trap[13].

I close the porthole and drag the heavy coffee table over, flipping it on its back across the hinged door. It would take an intruder with the strength of the hulk to push the flap open with the table on top of it. Even then, I'd at least wake up from the noise of the table shifting.

Settling in for the night under the mosquito net, I jump with each unfamiliar sound. The nocturnal noises of nature are shockingly loud. I identify the hum of cicadas and bird-like chirping from Tokay Geckos.

---

[13]Somehow, it never crossed my mind that leaving altogether was a valid option. I could have immediately checked out and found a more secure guesthouse in Canggu, yet I decided to stay and make an amateur booby trap.

To distract myself, I listen to a podcast. In this episode, the guest claims to have divine clairvoyance: the ability to communicate with angels. He believes anyone can do this, though, noting that angels send us signs all the time.

I glance up and notice the moonlight is projecting a pair of large, white angel wings onto the mosquito netting at the foot of my bed. I grab for my phone to snap a picture, just as he says, "and people often reach for their phone to take a picture, but it's like, you are in communication with the divine, put down the phone and communicate."

I have to chuckle at the coincidental timing.

"Okay, noted," I think as I rest my phone back down onto the mattress.

The guest encourages listeners to communicate with simple question statements, such as, "Angels, thank you for showing yourself to me. What do I need to know?"

With nothing to lose, I pause the podcast and repeat his question out loud. Within my head, I hear an immediate response reverberate back to me. It sounds like my own voice, the one that I hear when I think, but from a different part of my mind.

"You are safe, and you are protected."

I experienced this type of intuitive communication before, like when the tiny voice in my head clearly articulated, "I want to go to Bali," but even then, it said "I," indicating the thought was mine.

This is different.

The voice spoke directly to me, addressing me as "you," as if from an external position beyond my own thoughts and consciousness.

Was my overactive imagination playing tricks on me, mirroring the content of the podcast? Or was the divine actually in communication with me, offering a moment of reassurance?

I'm reminded of mindfulness teachings that discuss 'the watcher', a metaphor to describe our ability to observe thoughts and impulses as they arise, instead of acting on them. Eventually with practice, the watcher can help us notice how our thoughts lead to programmed emotional responses and behaviors, helping us detach and stop acting on 'auto-pilot'.

So, if the watcher is focusing inward, while our mind and thoughts are simultaneously focusing outward, who or what, is it? An expression of our own consciousness, or an expression of the divine? Perhaps, they are part and parcel of the same thing, like how a drop of water in the ocean is both an individual droplet and an inseparable part of the flow.

Either way, I'm relieved. Somehow, I intuitively know with resounding certainty there will be no intruders. I can sleep peacefully because something, or someone, is protecting me.

The next morning, I awake with the sun and sheepishly deconstruct my booby trap. I brew coffee and sit in silence, watching the light rise over the vast fields with profound gratitude. Smiling to myself, I close my eyes, feeling the warm light on my face.

I check out and order a Gojek to take me to a guesthouse in Canggu, where I'll be staying for the rest of the week.

The first thing I notice is the traffic: we are stuck in gridlock. When we begin to move again, my attention is drawn to my driver, who I realize for the first time appears to be quite old.

Out of nowhere, I feel an impulse to give him the 100,000 rupiah note in my wallet. Not as a tip or an act of charity; this is much stronger than that. It's as if the money already belongs to him, as if he'd dropped it by accident and I'm simply returning it.

My rational mind kicks in, reminding myself the taxi fare is only a quarter of this amount.

Still, I hear it over and over in my mind: a reverberant thought that I should give him the money.

Despite often approaching life with an analytical mind equipped with healthy skepticism, I've reached a point in my spiritual journey where I trust my intuition, even if it doesn't always make logical sense. It's what I referred to before as radical optimism or saying yes without considering the consequences of that yes. Rather than question the impulse of giving him the money, I surrender to it.

We reach the gate of my guesthouse, and I hand him the 100,000 bill. He reaches for his wallet to make change, and I quickly say, "no, it's for you."

He stares at me, confused.

I look him in the eyes and offer a polite smile. He appears to be mentally processing this unexpected turn of events and I notice a softening in his face, perhaps even a realization behind his eyes.

I sensed he had a greater purpose[14] for the money than whatever I would have spent it on. He might have even prayed for it that morning before accepting my ride, and if that were the case, I was merely part of a chain of events set in motion by a larger force. Was this the power of manifestation, the grace of God, or pure coincidence?

I thank him for the ride and walk through an opening in the gate.

---

[14]It's unnecessary and perhaps even inappropriate to tip this extravagantly, unless like me, you're inextricably compelled to give someone money. Like I said, it felt overwhelmingly like the money already belonged to him and I could not ignore the impulse I should 'give it back' to him. To this day, I have never experienced something like this again.

13

What if I fall?

Canggu is known for beach club parties, trendy restaurants and good surf, making it a popular spot for backpackers and digital nomads. I'm far past my party girl stage though, living more like an elderly woman who's in bed by 9:00pm. I avoid areas with booming night clubs and drunkards like the bubonic plague, so I chose to stay in the neighboring area of Pererenan for its reputation of being more quiet. Plus, it has its own beach and is close enough to Canggu that I can explore both areas while prioritizing my peace.

I'm staying at a family guesthouse managed by a Balinese woman called Nyoman. She shows me to my room, a cozy and simple space with a canopy bed and ensuite bathroom, and asks if I'd like assistance with renting a scooter.

"I would like to learn how to drive a scooter. Do you know a driving instructor?"

Within moments, I have a session scheduled for the following day with a man called Ketut.

In the meantime, I'm feeling sociable and decide to give the dating app another try. I match with Keeran, an Irish accountant also taking an extended career break in Bali. I share with him through instant message that I recently lived in Dublin, and we immediately click. He invites me for a morning rice field walk and we meet at a trendy café to grab coffees to go.

Keeran has a quiet, sweet demeanor. While we wait for our takeaway drinks, he tells me about his adventures in Thailand before arriving to Bali. He'd taken Thai kickboxing lessons, which in turn kicked his butt so bad he could barely walk for days. The memory sends Keeran into hysterics. He throws back his head, laughing so forcefully that spit flies from his mouth like a wet meteor, ricocheting off my forearm with shocking velocity.

Internally, I'm reeling that a stranger's bodily fluids are on my skin, but I keep a poker straight face to not embarrass him; though I suspect both of us are aware of what just happened. It takes every ounce of strength and moral fiber in my body to not reach for a napkin and wipe away the bead of spittle now resting comfortably in the baby hairs of my arm. I collect my iced coffee from the barista and casually wipe it on my skirt when Keeran's not looking.

We step outside into the sunshine and make a plan to stroll through a rice field near his guesthouse. Keeran insists on driving, so I climb up onto the back of his motorbike rental, a large and sporty looking N-Max. We teeter around angular, hairpin turns, and I silently hold my breath, clutching the back of the seat.

"This is the site of my accident," he calls back, as if reading my mind.

Shocked by this morsel of information, I only now notice the bandage on his left leg.

Jesus take the wheel!

We pull up to a parking area near his guesthouse and I clamber down, grateful to have two feet back on solid ground. I ask if his leg is okay, and he gravely shares in his Irish accent, "it's got a spot of infection".

Behind his guesthouse, there's a foot trail which circumvents a sprawling rice field. Palm trees line the periphery of the field and sway in the soft breeze. I pause and snap a photo while Keeran continues ahead.

I've just managed to stow my phone back in my purse before my reflexes kick into high gear. Something enters my field of vision, and I instinctively throw my arms overhead, feeling sharp pain in my hand. I release a startled scream.

"Ahhhh!"

Keeran whips around and finds me several steps behind, examining a cut on my hand. A coconut shell lays by my feet.

"A coconut nearly fell on my head…I threw my hands up just in time."

We glance up at the swaying palm trees overhead and exchange inextricable looks of disbelief. I begin to laugh, because what are the odds?

I don't feel a romantic connection with Keeran, but I enjoyed his company. He offers to drive me home but I'm insistent on taking a Gojek this time, rather hopeful to avoid adding any more injuries to my day. We hug goodbye and I turn to climb on my motorcycle taxi, thinking to myself: "I have got to learn how to drive a bike."

The next day, I'm introduced to Ketut, a middle-aged Balinese man with a kind smile. He collects me from my guesthouse, and I hop on the back of his scooter. We arrive at an empty parking lot where he will teach me to drive his Honda scoopy.

"Rule number one: always wear a helmet."

Ketut hands me a black bucket helmet resembling a mushroom, and I put it on, fumbling over the buckled chin strap. He straddles the scooter and demonstrates how to use both feet as kickstands.

"Like duck feet," he says playfully.

Ketut reminds me that anytime I feel unsteady, especially on sharp corners, I can simply slow the bike and put my feet down for balance. He explains the etiquette around honking and its importance when passing, driving in someone else's blind spot, or rounding blind corners. Finally, Ketut warns me to never reverse while the engine is on.

"Or else you go too fast, you go boom." He cackles in delight at the thought.

I confess to Ketut that I'm afraid of falling, mentally conjuring an image of Keeran's bandaged leg.

He tells me that it's true, some tourists crash because they are arrogant, they don't take the time to learn.

"Not you," he smiles. "You learn to drive the Balinese way!"

It's the moment of truth.

I mount the scooter and flick back the kickstand with my left foot before starting up the engine.

Ketut looks on with patient authority, "gentle now, slowly, slowly."

I ease the bike forward with both feet still on the ground like he showed me, building speed until I'm confident to lift them up. I make laps around the parking lot with a toothy grin on my face.

Ketut claps and cheers for me as I go for another round. "I knew you wouldn't fall!"

Ketut drops me back to the guesthouse and I'm suspended in a state of nostalgia.

I am six years old and terrified of riding a bicycle. Each time my parents suggest removing the training wheels, I resist.

One weekend, my Grandmother persuades me to try, assuring me she will hold the bike from behind, so I won't fall. She removes the training wheels and we go outside.

We slowly move forward together, and she releases her hands from the tiny bicycle frame without me noticing. I continue to ride straight and steady into the distance until I eventually notice she isn't there anymore.

I'm furious.

"You promised not to let go!" I exclaim, as angry tears slide down my tiny face.

"Yes," she admits, "but I knew you could do it."

She persuades me to try again, this time without her. I'm scared, unsure of my ability to do it on my own.

"But what if I fall?" I ask, worried.

"You might, but that's life. Sometimes we fall down, but we have to get back up, dust ourselves off and keep on trying."

I wobble at first, but catch my balance, building up speed and confidence.

I cheer in triumph, slowly arching around to return to her, noting a look of pride[15] on her face.

"See, I knew you wouldn't fall," she says, punctuating her grin with a wink.

"Come on, there's ice cream in the freezer. I got your favourite flavor, cotton candy."

---

[15]She's been gone for nearly ten years, but sometimes I swear she speaks to me, through me. I wonder if she's watching over me, if she's proud of who I've become. I hope wherever she is, she's okay —no, I hope she's better than okay, I hope she's free.

14

Who's Your Daddy?

I am severely addicted to caffeine.

A cup of coffee is usually my first thought when I wake up. The problem is, once I'm caffeinated, my mind becomes so energized that thoughts bounce off the ridges of my brain like stray ping pong balls, making meditation much more challenging. In Ubud, I formed a routine where coffee was a post-meditation reward, but my recent change in location has interrupted this habit.

I awake exhausted and immediately succumb to my caffeine cravings, abandoning my meditation practice entirely and reverting to an old habit of mindless scrolling on social media. As I open my phone, I see several notifications for the dating app and curiosity wins.

I have a new match with a guy called Jeff.

Jeff is an aspiring screenplay writer in Bali for a few weeks on a writing retreat. He is pictured smiling in a Hawaiian print button-up shirt with the buttons undone, revealing a bronzed chest and toned abs. The next photo shows him lounging by a pool wearing swim trunks sprinkled with pug faces with heart eyes. The next shows him holding a pug, who I assume is the muse for his board shorts in the previous photo. Next, he's holding a coffee in one hand and a leash in the other while walking his pug on a Gold Coast beach in Australia.

I tap open my inbox and read a greeting from Jeff.

"G'day Steph. I enjoyed your profile. You seem like a really interesting person. Would you like to get a drink later?"

I'm impressed with his direct communication. I noticed many of my matches never seemed to lead to an actual meet-up in real life. I had enough long-distance relationships with my friends and family back home to manage, so the last thing I wanted was a pen pal.

Plus, I learned the hard way with Keeran, that I could spend a lot of time and energy texting someone, but after meeting in person there just wasn't a romantic resonance. It seemed favorable to meet as soon as possible to gauge the dynamic in real life.

I accept Jeff's invitation, and we decide to meet at Pererenan beach at sunset.

Later, I walk outside to the red Honda scoopy scooter I've rented after my successful driving lesson with Ketut, and cautiously drive down the lane. I'm chronically lost and running late, so I leave early for my date even though the beach is just down the road. I arrive within minutes and am now far too early.

I park and meander over to our meet up spot: a large statue of a man riding a fish with an elephant head and scan the crowd of tourists lining the beach.

As I wait, a Balinese woman with a basket of bracelets approaches.

"Yes? Bracelet?"

I hesitate and she pounces.

"What's your name? Where you from?"

I tell her.

"Ohhh, I am Mary."

She tells me of the hard time she's experienced since the pandemic halted tourism in Bali, hinting that my purchase of a bracelet would significantly help her.

"Seashell bracelet maybe?" she asks, instinctively reaching for my wrist. I don't resist and once it's on my arm, I know there's no turning back.

"Yes, you looking so pretty. Matching anklet too?" she coos, glancing down at the bare ankle peeking out from my skirt. I fork over 100,000 rupiah for the set, far more than appropriate, but Mary is delighted.

"Thank you miss, thank you!" she says while stepping away. Just as her friend approaches with even more bracelets, I see Jeff and make a swift getaway.

Jeff is wearing the same Hawaiian print top from his profile photo, and he enthusiastically runs to me with a wide grin, reminding me of a Golden Retriever.

"Steph!" he exclaims excitedly in a thick Aussie accent, outstretching his long arms. He wraps me in a gentle hug, enveloping me in an aroma of clean linen and sandalwood. Jeff is tall; I have to crank my neck back to meet his gaze.

We walk towards the beach and flop into side-by-side bean bag chairs facing the water for the show—sunset that is—but the hordes of tourists also provide us with entertainment. We people watch while sipping nectar straight from ginormous green coconuts and conspiratorially wager which couples are on first dates, ironically unaware they might be doing the same to us. Jeff spouts off imaginary storylines for the beachgoers with ease. As a writer, I suppose these sorts of theatrics come natural to him.

Our conversation is effortless, and I find myself laughing genuinely. We talk about dating, the trials and tribulations of being single, and our dating 'icks'. Jeff remarks his approval of my punctuality: "I hate when people are late, it's disrespectful of my time."

I nod in agreement, silently aware that I have a propensity for running late, rather than on time. The sun dips under the horizon line and we admire the pastel shades of orange and pink that streak the sky.

"Steph, I'm enjoying myself. Would you like to go get a bite to eat somewhere else?"

I agree and we walk to our parked bikes.

He tells me he knows a place nearby and I follow him to a tiny eatery with tiki bar decor and picnic tables beneath strings of twinkling fairy lights.

We both order veggie burgers and soda waters, and remark on our shared hiatus from animal products and alcohol. He tells me he's struggling with an early morning writing routine, hence the avoidance of drink, and I tell him of my struggles with my own early morning routine meditating.

"I can see that the break from alcohol is working for you Steph, your eyes are glowing!"

I smile, absentmindedly stirring the ice in my drink with a straw. I feel comfortable around Jeff and find myself sharing my own aspirations of becoming an author. I tell him about my travel journals and my intuition that the content of my future book resides in the pages, which cascades into a long monologue about stationary.

"When I choose a journal, it's GOT to be a soft notebook without spiral binding, those are the worst…and each one's chosen intuitively by its 'vibe', so naturally each of my journals are a different color to represent that trip or chapter of my life. Actually, now that I think about it, the same goes for pens, which I'm sure you understand as a writer…if it doesn't write well, I won't like how it looks on the page and therefore whatever I write down is garbage, but tearing out a page is equally undesirable because then I have those ugly jagged pieces in the page line."

I only realize I sound neurotic after my verbal diarrhea and by then, the damage is done. Jeff politely let me yap on about writing implements, but his body language has changed. He's now leaning forward with his elbows on the table, fingers tented together, with a neutral expression on his face. His eyes narrow and seem to be sizing me up.

"Anyways, enough about stationary," I say with a giggle, eager to fill the silence that now suspends over our table.

Jeff relaxes into a less intense posture and throws his head back with a loud bark of a laugh.

"Steph, you are adorable."

My dimpled grin seems to have neutralized the unsolicited rampage about notebooks.

I'm prepared to pay for my own meal, aware that writers are usually not an inherently wealthy bunch. I'd feel uncomfortable having a starving artist pay for me. Growing up with a single parent in a modest home has made me considerate of such things.

Besides, I don't particularly like men paying for first dates. My awful interaction with creepy Matt has me second guessing whether they expect something in return. If I don't want a second date, it layers on an additional level of anxiety, as if I've used them for a free meal.

Jeff immediately grabs for the bill when it's placed on the table, so I don't resist.

"Jeff, this was so lovely. Thank you for dinner."

We end the evening with sentiments of an enjoyable evening and share a goodbye hug that forces my face into his under-arm, which thankfully was not too damp or smelly. I strap on my purple mushroom helmet and cautiously edge onto the road, shaking the armpit faceplant from my mind. I have bigger concerns of getting myself home in one piece on the dark back roads.

The next morning, I blink my eyes open to a bright room and reach for my phone on the bedside table. It's just after 8:00am and I have a text from Jeff.

"Hi Steph. So great to meet you yesterday! Do you have any plans tonight? I know a great Indonesian restaurant."

I have literally zero plans.

We agree on dinner at 'Casa Tua' at 7:00pm.

Fiending for a coffee, I skip morning meditation in favor of devotion of the cappuccino kind, relocating to a cafe called 'Front'. The first sip of a good cup of coffee sparks happy hormones in my brain, so I'm genuinely excited when I notice their industrial sized espresso machine.

I settle down in a corner booth with my drink and journal, popping ear buds in and becoming lost in my own world. I barely notice when the barista approaches my table, staring down at me. I glance up and take one ear bud out.

"You have red scoopy?" he asks.

It takes me a moment to register that he's referring to my rental scooter.

I notice a nervous looking blonde guy standing in the background, staring sheepishly at me.

"Hi, do you have the red Honda parked out front?" he cautiously asks, in a voice barely louder than a whisper.

"Yes..."

"I'm so sorry, but I knocked it over and there is some damage. I think you'd better come with me."

Oh god.

I slide out of the booth and follow him outside. From a distance, I see my red scooter sitting upright but with the front wheels at a violently crooked angle. I know I pulled in and parked straight. It's not until we get closer that I notice a large crack in the frame.

Did he knock it over or send it flying into another dimension?

I examine the crack and glance back at the guy, taking him in fully. He is tall, scrawny and looks to be around 20. His hands tremble as he points to the damage.

"Are you okay?"

"Yes," he says quietly.

"I was trying to back up, but I accidentally went forwards instead of backwards."

I immediately think of Ketut and his ominous warning to never reverse with the engine on. "You go too fast and go boom!"

Indeed Ketut, indeed.

"Well, the important thing is that you're not hurt. Thank you for your honesty, we will sort this out, don't worry," I tell him.

Truthfully, I hadn't considered what would happen in the case of an accident when renting my scooter. The rental terms were exceedingly casual: just a cash payment. I call Komang, the Balinese woman I've rented the scooter from, and relay to her the incident. She tells me to wait there.

Komang lives around the corner and arrives within five minutes. She's soft-spoken and does not appear upset. I wager this is not her first rodeo dealing with tourists crashing motorbike rentals. She crouches down by the bike and takes a photo of the damage.

Komang and Vlad, the guy who yeeted my bike, settle on an amount of 1 million rupiah to cover the cost of repairs.

Vlad pulls out a velcro wallet to offer her cash and I notice his hands trembling. He is clearly shaken from the incident and strangely, I feel protective of him. I thank him again for his honesty and ask if he will be okay to drive.

"Yes. Sorry again for your bike."

He seems eager to escape the situation and I watch him walk towards a sporty N-Max that appears humongous next to his skinny frame. The bike is identical to Keeran's, and I'm reminded of his bandaged leg with a 'spot of infection'.

I keep a straight face, but wince internally as Vlad climbs onto the large bike. A novice driver on such a powerful motorbike is like putting a toddler on a treadmill at full speed: it's not going to end well.

Vlad slowly edges the bike onto the road and lurches forward before sharply breaking to regain control. I'm genuinely afraid for him and those in his proximity. Embarrassment exudes from him like a fine mist. He keeps his eyes down and tries again with less throttle this time, slowly pulling away from the cafe.

Meanwhile, Komang appears content after receiving payment for the damages. She turns on my scooter and does a quick loop to make sure it's safe to drive, before handing me back the keys.

On the bright side, if I were to cause any scratches to the frame, it won't seem bad in comparison.

I walk back inside, and the barista looks up with a face registering both concern and curiosity. I give him a thumbs up sign, signaling that it's all good, and settle back in my booth.

My coffee is cold and I'm feeling less devotional.

Back at the guesthouse, I've lost track of time and rush to get ready for my dinner date with Jeff. I hope he's okay with a windswept, beachy look because I don't have time to do my hair or makeup. I change into a clean sundress and slide on my new seashell bracelet and anklet.

Pulling up the directions on my phone, I breathe a sigh of relief: I'm still on track to make it to the restaurant for 7:00pm.

What I didn't account for, was getting lost.

As a novice scooter driver myself, it requires so much mental focus to get around safely, that I'm incapable of simultaneously navigating. I also can't take directions from Siri through ear buds, because I never seem to react quick enough and end up missing turn after turn. Instead, I memorize the route before leaving: right onto the main road, a quick left and another right.

I take a wrong turn almost immediately and end up driving in the wrong direction on a major roadway, trying not to panic when nothing looks familiar and cars whip by at an alarming speed.

Where am I?

I pull off into a gas station and check my map. My heart drops when I realize I've unintentionally drove ten minutes in the wrong direction. I now vividly recall the dating ick Jeff disclosed to me.

"I hate when people are late, it's disrespectful of my time".

Shit.

It will be 7:00pm by the time I make it back to my starting point, and then I still need to get to the restaurant.

Hot prickles radiate across my skin. Suddenly the map doesn't make sense anymore and I struggle to orient where I am, in relation to which way I need to go.

I take a deep breath.

"Calm down Stephanie, it's not that big of a deal, just get there safely," I chastise myself while starting up the engine.

I backtrack and finally pull into the parking area in front of Casa Tua twenty-five minutes late.

I'm mortified.

I can see Jeff through the doorway, sitting at a table in the back garden, patiently waiting but looking dejected.

"Jeff!" I exclaim when I approach him with a hint of panic.

"I'm so sorry, I got lost."

He meets my eyes and seems to register my anxiety.

"Are you okay?"

"Yes," I look down, "but I remembered you saying you hate when people are late. I feel horrible."

He is silent, as if pondering this, and suddenly breaks out into a loud laugh.

"Yes, well I'm glad you're here now. I was beginning to think I was getting stood up. I hope you don't mind, but I ordered a few different vegetarian things, I thought we could share."

I relax and settle into my seat across from him. A waiter arrives with several dishes and Jeff asks for two side plates. We pick up where we left off and conversation flows easily, as we tuck into tender strips of tofu and veggies baked in folded parcels of banana leaves, skewers with savory tempeh, and urab sayur, a vegetable salad with coconut and chiles.

I excuse myself to use the restroom, a unisex space adjacent to the dining room. Before I can even close the door behind me, I see a sight that gives me such a jump scare that my soul might have left my body. I jump so high I might be levitating, and my hand protectively flounces over my chest like an elderly woman.

I hear boisterous laughter behind me and glance back towards the dining room. The owner, a Balinese guy, is howling at my expense while pointing his index finger at me for the entire dining room to see.

Jeff looks on with confusion.

Standing in the corner of the restroom, staring eerily towards the toilet with large red eyes, is a life-sized replica of the Jigsaw killer from the horror movie 'Saw'. The owner is now laughing so hard he wipes tears from his eyes, thoroughly enjoying himself. I close the door and force myself to get over my irrational stage fright with a murderous ventriloquist watching me 'take care of business'.

After dinner, Jeff suggests a night cap of mocktails.

I agree on the caveat that he navigates, cracking a joke at my own expense that I'd only lead us into a ditch. He knows I'm staying in the Pererenan neighborhood, so he suggests a place closer to my guesthouse, so I won't get lost driving home.

He says this earnestly, not sarcastically, and I'm grateful.

I strap on my purple helmet and Jeff smiles at me.

"You must be the only person on the planet that actually looks cute in one of those things."

I follow him to a trendy restaurant called 'Woods' and we sit at a corner booth, admiring a full-sized, living tree inside the dining room. We sit side-by-side with our heads tilted close together to hear one another over the music and chatter.

I'm facing a table with two ladies and our eyes meet several times. They hold their gaze and whisper to each other conspiratorially. I glance to Jeff and then back to the ladies, who are now giggling.

"Is it just me, or are they staring at us?"

Jeff seems to have noticed too and says, "Ermm, I think they may have recognized me."

Excuse me?

Unsure what he means, or how to respond, I silently wait for an explanation.

"I was in a movie a while back, when I lived in L.A., and um, sometimes this happens."

I think back to our first conversation.

Jeff told me he used to live in the US before recently moving back to Australia with his dog. He told me he was working on a screenplay but downplayed it to the extent that I assumed he was just breaking into the industry. I even worried about him paying for my veggie burger and soda.

Does he mean to tell me that all this time, he's been a movie star, and I just never recognized him? I'm both surprised and intrigued.

"Oh…anything I might have seen?"

He shares the name of his most recent action flick, and I draw a blank. I've never cared much for the action genre, so I'm forced to admit that I haven't seen it. I leave out the part that I've never heard of it.

When I'm back at my guesthouse later that night, I cannot resist searching the movie. Sure enough, he pops up as one of the lead roles, a rippling fighter character. Now privy to his full name on the cast list, I follow down a rabbit hole of his past acting gigs: a character in the TV series 'House of Lies' and a supporting role in the comedic film 'Anchor Man'.

The jig is up Jeff.

The next morning, I check out of my guesthouse with plans to return to Ubud. Jeff invites me for a final coffee to say goodbye before I head out. We meet at a beachfront cafe in Canggu called 'The Lawn' and order oat milk lattes, which I allow him to pay for as I'm now confident that he's far from a starving artist.

We cheers with paper takeaway cups and Jeff makes a toast.

"Steph, this was so unexpected but in the best way possible. What are the odds that a girl from Canada and a boy from Australia bump into each other on an island in the Indian Ocean? These strange collisions in life can have an impact far beyond the physical time spent together... You are one of those people for me. I'll always think fondly of this time and of that gorgeous Canadian girl I met in Bali."

While Jeff appears to be a gentlemanly character that seems to say 'all the right things', his speech—inclusive of glistening eyes—feels a bit theatrical. Now that I know he's an actor, I'm slightly skeptical of his passionate words that seem disproportionate to the three days we've known each other.

Theatrics aside, we seem to share an unspoken agreement that this is the end of the road for us. After all, he lives in Australia and I don't. Trying to force a brief vacation romance to be anything more, would only complicate things and inevitably taint our perceptions of one another. If we leave things exactly as they are now, it would be just like Jeff put it: a fond memory[16].

I look up into his eyes and he brushes away an unruly tress of hair from my face. He leans in, cupping my head with his hand and I stand on my tip-topes to reach him. Our lips briefly meet in a sweet, sentimental kiss that would be our first and last.

"Take care Steph."

He looks into my eyes, pausing for a moment, as if about to say something more. I take a step back.

"Goodbye Jeff."

---

[16]A year later, I stumbled across a scandalous tabloid article exposing Jeff for adultery and a 'daddy dominatrix' fetish. It turned out Jeff had a long-term girlfriend the entire time and I was not the only woman he dated during that trip to Bali, despite his warm sentiments about our shared time together (*rolls eyes*). One of his other Bali romances progressed into a one-year, long distance relationship, where he coerced her to participate in his kink—until she found out about his double life and exposed him publicly. It's safe to say I dodged a bullet. No, I dodged a daddy sized bazooka.

15

American Dick

Kedak, the taxi driver who collected me from the airport when I first arrived in Bali has now become my go-to driver for long distance rides. He picks me up from the guesthouse in Pererenan and we slowly make our way back to Ubud.

Bali is not exactly set up for commuters or heavy traffic. Most roads are narrow and winding, making it difficult to pass slowly crawling trucks or tourist minivans. Two hours later, we turn past Warung Ting Ting and slowly edge down the back lane that converges into a sidewalk.

I pay Kedak and walk the rest of the way, retracing familiar steps to the fork in the path. This time I do not turn left as it sharply veers towards my old jungle flat but continue straight to the adjacent property: my new house sit.

Ana receives me warmly and shows me the practical things in the home, like lights and locks, in between packing for her flight back to Makassar.

I settle into my new room, where my suitcase has been awaiting my return. I find Neo napping on the bed and offer him a gentle stroke across his soft head as a greeting. He flicks open his blue eyes and registers me with indifference, before curling up and falling asleep again. I'm grateful to unpack my belongings into an eight-foot wardrobe, a small luxury after living out of a suitcase for two years.

Ana pops her head through my open door:

"I'm heading down to Cafe Vespa for a bite to eat and will catch my taxi to the airport there. Would you care to join me?"

I suddenly realize that I'm starving.

We walk together down the concrete path, stopping along the way to greet the neighborhood dogs, who run to Ana as if they are long lost friends. She affectionately coos at a fluffy puppy who appears from an alley to our right. "Hello Beans! Are you a silly little dog? Yes, you are!"

The main corner of the village is positioned at a small four-way crossing, with a bridge to the left leading up to the popular Yellow Flower Cafe. Vespa is to the right, situated at the corner of the junction. We walk in and Ana sees several people she knows. She introduces me to Dean, a soft-spoken writer with a man bun; Myles, an outgoing retreat leader with shaggy brown hair; and Rachel, an elegant small business owner with long lashes and glowing skin.

The scene is reminiscent of the famed New York cafe from the set of Friends. It sounds like during the pandemic, Cafe Vespa became a community hub for the expats here, including this tight-knit group of friends.

"Vespa was one of the only places that stayed open during the lockdowns, so it became our spot," they tell me.

Ana mentions that I will be house and cat sitting for her and wonders if the crew can take me under their wings while she's gone. Dean suggests a group outing the following night for live music here at Vespa. We exchange numbers over a lunch of pumpkin dosa and shortly after, Ana's taxi arrives. I excuse myself at the same time as a wave of fatigue washes over me from my day of travel and moving in.

I return home and let myself in with my new house key, finding three hungry cats waiting for dinner. Each has their own tiny dish, which I fill with scoops of kibble. Neo eats the fastest, moving on for stolen seconds from timid Echo's plate. She looks at him with indignation before strutting away, leaving him to feast.

My bedroom has an outdoor ensuite bathroom and I've been asked to leave the door open, so the cats can get in and out when the front door is locked. I have a mosquito net over my canopy bed so I'm content with this arrangement, eagerly looking forward to an evening cross-breeze.

It's apparent that a feline has been in here while we were gone. There's a tiny welcome present waiting on the foot of my bed: a bird's intestinal tract sprinkled with feathers.

Ana also left me the keys to her grey Honda Scoopy, so the next evening I drive myself down to Cafe Vespa, taking great caution not to veer off the narrow cement track into the rice paddies below.

Darkness falls like a black veil over Ubud around 6:30pm and I arrive at dusk, parking the scooter out front. I find Dean inside, joined by an American couple and the owner, a thin, middle-aged man with round rimmed spectacles. The American woman and the owner apparently knew each other when they both lived in China.

"It's like a lifetime ago," she says dreamily.

I'm stuck beside her goofy husband, a balding man about my age in elephant print pajama pants and a tank top emboldened with a bronze Ganesha, the elephant God.

I sit across from Dean, and we lean over the table to hear each other over the live music.

"So, how long have you guys been together?" the American man asks us.

We glance at each other, embarrassed and uncertain how to respond. Dean diplomatically replies, "I'm flattered you'd think that, but we're just friends. We actually just met."

"Ohhh cool," the man says, obnoxiously throwing his head back with a loud giggle reminiscent of Janice from Friends. He seems oblivious to the awkwardness he just thrust upon us.

The conversation swiftly turns in a far more bizarre direction, as the woman recounts the linguistic skills she learned in China: predominantly naughty words. She teaches us how to say penis in Mandarin, though Dean and I do not participate in the lesson, silently watching on with perplexion.

The word penis seems to have sparked a phallus-related memory in her husband, who begins to brag about their son's member, an appendage that is apparently disproportionate to his tiny body.

"It's been like that since he came out of the womb, you should have seen this thing when he was born," the man exclaims with pride.

To my horror, he proceeds to whip out his phone and open his picture album, rapidly scrolling through images to find one from the delivery room. He shoves the phone in my face, keenly watching for a reaction. Dean is rendered silent, looking on in slack-mouthed shock.

"Well…I'm afraid I haven't seen many naked babies, so I don't have much to compare it to."

The man looks disappointed by my response and stows the phone back in his pajama pants pocket.

My eyes flick to Dean and we exchange a brief look. I'm relieved when he starts a new conversation, and we discuss his upcoming trip to Nepal.

Guzzling down a mocktail to mitigate my awkwardness, I realize this is the type of event I normally rely on alcohol to get me through, downing pints of beer to damper my social anxiety. Now sober, I'm introverted and viscerally aware of the array of sounds and smells around me: the music and hum of voices, forks scraping on plates, cigarette smoke drifting in from outside, clinking glasses and the whir of traffic from the road.

I struggle to hear Dean and am forced to sit mute and uncomfortable with the void of conversation. Worse, the man beside me continually leans into my space, yelling into my ear. I notice a piece of meat wedged between his crooked teeth. He's not eating, so I wonder how long it's been there. Prickles of heat spread through my body, and I glance away before I gag.

Occasionally, I experience something I call my 'escape reflex': an excruciatingly urgent desire to leave when I've reached my maximum limit of socialization. My options are to immediately escape, usually by way of an Irish exit, or to stay and endure rising anxiety that can turn into a panic attack. The latter option typically appears to others like a winding down; a gradual progression of my outgoing demeanor into a more quiet and tired one. Or it can happen quickly and seemingly out of nowhere, like a TV turning off, prompting questions of the 'are you okay?' variety.

No, I'm not okay, but I'll never admit it.

Alcohol thwarts this need to escape, taking the edge off my incessant over-thinking. I contemplate ordering a glass of red wine, but quickly catch the thought in its tracks. I have reached four months of sobriety and do not want to ruin my progress.

While I hate to abandon Dean before the music is even over, I ask for my vegetarian pizza in a takeaway box and make an excuse to leave early.

I'm home before 9:00pm.

16

In My Health Era

The Balinese rice paddies are highly romanticized and glamorized on social media. A rice field walk has even become a 'must do' experience when on a trip to Bali. Living next to a rice field has a different reality than what's posted online though.

First of all, the lush green aesthetic is seasonal. The crops will inevitably disappear once the rice is harvested, leaving behind a mucky, razored field. In the process, farmers will be farming.

It's currently pre-harvest season and hungry birds descend upon the crops as if dining at an open buffet. While I've seen some scarecrows clad in upcycled garments or an old motorcycle helmet, the stewards of the land I'm staying on have a rather innovative method to prevent crop loss.

A long strip of tin, thicker than foil but much thinner than sheet metal, hangs in the air from a string horizontally spanning the field. The same device is rigged up on the adjacent field so the farmer can simultaneously tug each string from a middle point, making the tin pieces dance like a marionette. Metal violently bending against wind makes a joltingly loud noise, startling the birds and anyone else in the vicinity.

The bird scaring device is approximately five meters from my bedroom window, so really there's no need for an alarm clock. If the shaking foil doesn't wake me, the farmer's callous crow imitations do the trick.

"Haahhh, haahhh."

I rise and head to the open-air kitchen, surprised when tiny Neva does not come outside for breakfast. She's often the first to come running when I shake the container filled with kibble. I find her hiding under my bed with something dark wedged in her jaws: Neva has a bat.

She sees me and runs, attempting to make an escape. I'm worried she will shred the poor thing and leave it on my bed as a gift, so I snatch her from behind before she manages to dart away. I carry her—bat still in mouth—with outstretched arms, like Mufasa presenting Simba to all of Pride Rock. Outside now, she squirms out of my grasp, simultaneously dropping the bat onto the tiles adjacent to the pool. The bat lays immobile and she pounces. It takes off into flight just in time, but only manages to hover a meter from the ground like a butterfly.

Neva jumps vertically with outstretched claws.

"FLY!" I scream.

"Flyyyyyyyy little guy!"

The bat has a sudden burst of energy and takes off into the sky.

I cheer, suddenly ecstatic for its safe escape. Neva makes an audible cry of disappointment, reminding me of a child whose toy is taken away. She saunters off to the kitchen for breakfast and I join her to make a smoothie.

Today I have a highly undesirable medical appointment: a check-up with a gynecologist.

My Canadian doctor's receptionist previously left several voicemail messages, reminding me to come in for the preventative screening test for cervical cancer. As I'm not in the country, I hadn't returned her calls and she's resorted to emailing me.

Now that I'm settled at the house sit, my attention returns to the 'complete health overhaul' I swore to adopt during my first month in Bali. I reluctantly book myself into a highly rated women's clinic in Denpasar. I never dreamed this is how I'd be spending my time in Bali, but I'm a brand-new woman prioritizing her health.

I've asked Kedak to take me to Denpasar and back. He usually waits for me at the lane-to-sidewalk junction, but today I suggest he collects me from Ubud Coffee Roastery, a new shop that's popped up kitty-corner to Cafe Vespa. It's a slightly further walk for me through the village, but I want a coffee for the one-hour drive.

As I'm walking, I see Dean approach on his motorbike; he slows to say hello.

"Steph! How are you? I felt so bad you left the live music early, that guy was so rude!"

Dean must have assumed I left due to the bizarre interaction with the phallic obsessed American, and in part, he is correct.

I chuckle and nod.

"He was certainly an interesting individual."

"You are too nice Steph. He was a real asshole."

I laugh again, nodding in silent agreement.

"How is work going?" I ask. Dean is a freelance writer juggling several columns, in addition to his own blog.

"Ohhh yah know, just another day in paradise."

I'm unsure if he's being sarcastic or not, seeing as we quite literally do live in a paradise, so I smile broadly in response. Dean glances over his shoulder and notices another scooter approaching.

"Steph, it was lovely bumping into you."

"Definitely. See you around!"

I pop into Ubud Coffee Roastery and order an oat milk latte to go, settling down onto the concrete steps outside to wait for Kedak.

We arrive at the women's health clinic an hour later and I walk through glass doors into a blast of cold air. The clinic is exceedingly clean, with white floors that reflect off the bright overhead lights. A polite receptionist checks me in and directs me to a white leather couch to wait.

The doctor, a middle-aged Balinese man, calls me into an examination room the size of a large walk-in closet.

"You can change into the skirt and place your clothes in the white box," he instructs before exiting the room.

The white box is on a metal trolley containing medical equipment. Did he mean for me to place my dirty shoes and clothes next to sterile implements?

My brain momentarily glitches as I overthink his instructions, doubting whether I understood correctly. To air on the safe side, I leave my shoes on the floor beside the trolley, neatly piling my folded trousers and underwear on top of them.

I step into the skirt, which is a loose slip approximately ten sizes too big and notice a padded chair in a reclined position.

I'm used to the exam beds in North America, covered with crinkly hygiene paper that reminds me of parchment lining on a baking sheet. Back home, they have stainless steel stirrups at the end of the bed, like foot pedals on a spin bike, but this is like nothing I've seen. These stirrups are long, more closely resembling the shape of a hotdog.

I sit gingerly on the edge of the recliner, struggling to lift my feet into the hotdogs. I manage it but am forced into a maximum squat position that is difficult for my tight hips. It looks like I'm hovering over a drop toilet.

I hear a knock on the door.

The doctor enters without glancing up. He sits on a wheeled stool at a desk in the corner, preparing the equipment.

He swivels over to find me squatted and hunched over like a gargoyle perched on the roof of a building. I'm teetering on the edge of the chair with both feet resting atop the oval foot holds.

"Oh...can I help you?"

He looks genuinely concerned.

He asks me to sit back and gently slides my feet down the hot dog shaped stirrups, which I now realize are not foot holds; they are meant to support the lower legs.

My calves now rest comfortably, but my social anxiety does not: I feel like a freak.

The doctor is extremely discrete, and the entire process is complete in mere moments, a far superior experience to reproductive healthcare in Canada[17].

Kedak is waiting out front for me. I pay at reception and climb into the van, immediately deflating. It's as if all my energy was on reserve for that single appointment, and now that it's over, I'm utterly depleted. We ride back to Ubud in silence, while I stare out the window. The rest of the week seems to blur in a similar state of moody introversion.

---

[17]The exam cost $40 USD, and I received my lab results back the next day via WhatsApp messenger. This is a staggering difference from Canada, where it can take months just to get an appointment and even longer receive results via snail mail.

17

Fish n Chips Lips

Kedak slowly winds the vehicle around hairpin turns along the eastern coastline of Bali. We climb the Maha Gangga valley, which offers an expansive view of plummeting rice fields beneath dramatic clouds that resemble charcoal streaks on a white canvas.

Ana is back from Makassar, and I have a weekend away from the cats to explore the Northeastern part of the island. Once a sleepy fishing village, Amed is now a popular tourist destination for those wishing to escape the chaos of the busy South. It's well known among scuba divers for its access to shipwrecks, which is why I've come.

I'm staying in a family-owned guesthouse within walking distance to Lipah Beach, a quiet bay tucked further down the coastline. The property manager leads me down a concrete path with several side-by-side bungalows.

I have a front porch with a lounge chair and coffee table, but don't anticipate that I will use them: directly across is a building under construction. Hammering and drilling was definitely not in the property description, nor aligned with my expectations of a peaceful stay, but I'm only here for a few nights and I've already paid.

"I'll have to make do," I think, grateful for remembering to pack my noise canceling headphones.

Inside my room, there's a bamboo framed bed, a writing desk and a wardrobe. I unpack and rest my laptop on the desk. I have a Zoom call to chat with an old colleague from the University in Ireland. She asked if I'm interested in picking up work, and while I'm mixed about it, my bank account could use the boost.

As I prepare for our call to discuss the project and what would be involved, loud music starts playing next door. Speakers alternate between bass-blasting beats and microphone amplified voices belting out renditions of 90s pop tunes. While my colleague knows I'm in Bali and that I'd work remotely from here, I'm still concerned by taking the call with such a boisterous background, including ear-piercing karaoke.

I decide to find a quieter—albeit a public—space to take the call and relocate to a Warung down the road. I order a soda water with ice and open my laptop, tethering it to the hotspot on my phone. Two little Balinese girls playing in the back of the Warung have noticed me. They inch closer and peer around my shoulder with curiosity, unintentionally photo-bombing the call that's now in progress. The girls gather courage and peep directly into the screen, giggling and dancing now, wildly undulating their tiny limbs in joy.

Their Mom comes over to wrangle them away, pausing to also peer into the laptop. The three of them now sit together behind me, watching and simultaneously being watched by my colleague through the screen.

"We have an audience," I joke.

A feral tom cat enters the cafe and jumps onto my table, screeching for food. He tip-toes in front of my laptop, obstructing the camera with streaks of orange fur. The cat is our breaking point and now the entire scene is hilarious. We both collapse into a fit of giggles. We settle on a part-time six-month research contract to start in a few weeks.

I power down my laptop and celebrate with generous portions of Nasi Goreng, vegetarian fried rice, and Gado Gado, a platter of hard-boiled eggs, coconut salad and steamed veggies. The cat is now under the table, and I toss him scraps of tempeh and egg, which he gobbles up with shocking speed.

The next morning, I'm booked to go scuba diving at the WWII Liberty shipwreck in Tulamben, another fishing village 40 minutes Northeast of Amed. I arrive with my dive master, Putu, a young Balinese man with a mischievous demeanor and boisterous laugh. The dive site has a shore entrance, which involves wading into the water with our heavy scuba gear until it's deep enough to descend.

I tug on my wetsuit and sit on a bench to suit up, strapping on my BCD vest and oxygen tank, flippers and mask before shuffling like a penguin over the gravelly coastline. I've not even entered the water and am unstable on my feet, struggling against the weight of the tank, so I'm skeptical when I notice the choppy waves. They're fiercely strong and within seconds I'm on my ass, floundering in ankle deep water like a beached whale. Putu is much steadier and helps me up, clamping down on my forearm the way a parent might grab a toddler who's just tried to run off.

We're waist deep now and the waves relentlessly hammer into us, pushing us backwards and knocking our tanks together. Putu gives me a thumbs down sign indicating it's time to descend and we release the air in our vests, escaping under the waves and skimming across the sand bar to a steep drop off.

We slowly descend to 22 meters and glide towards the shipwreck, a dilapidated skeleton of a boat resting on the bottom at a crooked angle. The vessel is massive, at almost one hundred meters from bow to stern. We barely manage to circumvent its exterior before needing to return to the surface to swap out our air tanks.

On our second dive, we explore the inside of the wreck, drifting through a large opening towards the helm. Putu floats in front of the steering wheel, which is immaculately intact, and pretends to rotate his arms back and forth to turn the ship. He makes a rectangular shape with his hands and clicks his index finger, motioning for me to move into position at the wheel for a photo. I float forward and pantomime steering the wheel for the underwater camera.

We squeeze through a narrow passage, leading to an interior space that is so dark it emanates an eerie, blue shade. It's spooky in here and I wonder whether lives were lost in this wreck, but quickly shake the morbid thought from my mind.

Edging forward towards the exit, we enter a tunnel-like hole illuminated by sunlight and…suddenly I'm yanked backwards by the hose feeding me oxygen. Instinctively, I clamp my jaw and bite down on the regulator, so it's not ripped from my mouth. I pause and slowly inch forward with no result.

I'm stuck.

I trace my fingers along the hose from my mouth to behind my shoulder and feel a thick bundle of seaweed. The visceral signs of my escape reflex are looming, but I cannot simply leave this situation. Even if I wasn't caught on seaweed, bolting to the surface can cause a serious dive injury. We are so deep that we must do a mandatory 3-minute safety stop before fully ascending to prevent nitrogen bubbles forming in our blood.

I simply cannot panic down here—it could be life or death.

Taking a slow, deep breath, I force my hand through the knot of seaweed, releasing it from the regulator hose. I notice Putu's face appear from the other end of the tunnel, but I no longer need his help. With relief, I kick my flippers and glide forward to reach him, entering open water infused with beams of light from the surface.

Back on land, my adrenaline turns into euphoria, and I book another dive before fear can talk me out of it.

The next day, I have lunch at a restaurant called Blue Earth and meet a Kiwi named Will. We connected on the dating app, and both happen to be in Amed for scuba diving, though he's also taking a free diving course hosted at the restaurant. We briefly chat while he's on break from the course programming and agree to meet up for dinner later to swap dive stories.

Will has a rental motorbike and drives to meet me at a Warung in Lipah Beach near my guesthouse. There's a live band and unfortunately, the only remaining table is directly in front of the singer. Similar to my experience with Dean and the phallic-obsessed American man, conversation proves to be a challenge over the loud music. I'm forced to ask Will to repeat himself two or three times until we give up entirely during the songs, silently bobbing along to the singer's renditions of classics.

It is excruciatingly awkward.

In the absence of conversation, I have a strange sense of 'being on display'. I micromanage my facial expressions, methodically rotating my eyes from the singer to random objects in the room and back to Will. We eagerly share brief exchanges in the quiet spaces between songs, until finally the performer finishes his set.

Thank God.

Our meals come out around the same time, and I distract myself with food. Will is shier than I expected, and our conversation is forced, requiring more effort on my part to continually think of new things to say. It's not that I feel the need to fill every moment with conversation. I quite enjoy silence, but I guess I'm just uncomfortable in silence with Will.

In my mind, I'm also battling an unrelenting obsessive thought that I have spinach in my teeth. This is not uncommon for me, starting as a teen with braces. They were quite literally 'metal food catchers' and it was a source of embarrassment and social anxiety. All these years later, the compulsion to check my teeth after eating remains. Most of the time though, I don't find anything lodged in my gumline, so I resist the urge to excuse myself from the table to check in the bathroom. Instead, I silently practice mindfulness techniques, allowing the thoughts to rise and fall with observant neutrality.

Will points out that it's a full moon and suggests a walk on the beach. I peg him as trustworthy and feel safe in going alone with him. Walking on the beach at night is not something I would do alone as a solo woman, so I pounce on the opportunity to be accompanied by Will.

We stroll to the edge of the water and sit side-by-side in the sand, where conversion flows a little easier. I don't feel a romantic resonance with Will, and I think the feeling is mutual: there isn't an overly flirtatious vibe and neither of us inches closer.

I'm reaching my escape reflex and tell Will I have an early dive scheduled as an excuse to end the date. He offers to walk me back to my guesthouse and I gratefully accept, preferring not to walk alone at night on poorly lit roads. We reach my gate and Will hovers, not saying anything but looking as if he wants to.

"Would you want to come back with me to my hotel for

the night…as friends?"

I'm shocked.

Not only had I just told him I have an early start tomorrow to end the date—rather than express interest in extending it—but there were zero indications the night was leading up to this. There was no flirtatious banter, no hand holding or even kissing that would suggest the possibility of a hook-up. All signs lead to the friend zone, though it seems Will is on the same page, framing his proposition as friends with benefits.

Thrown off, I stammer an awkward response.

"I…um…I think I'm good."

My eyes flick to his and register a disappointed look on his face that incites resentment within me. It was an incredibly awkward date with forced conversation; surely that could not have been a one-sided experience. So, what gave him the impression this was a possibility?

"Goodnight Will," I say firmly.

I walk away, silently cursing myself for being so bloody awkward, while also feeling angry that he put me in this uncomfortable position in the first place. I get inside and lock the door behind me, sighing with relief to be alone again.

While getting ready for bed, I pause in front of the mirror, audibly groaning in embarrassment: there is a leafy chunk of spinach wedged between my two front teeth. It's so big it could only go unnoticed by someone legally blind. A visceral wave of mortification that I can only describe as the 'heebie-jeebies', washes over me, adding to the awkwardness of the evening. My discomfort is so strong, I'm rendered nauseous. To relieve the tension in my body, I shake my arms as if trying to rid my hands of invisible droplets of water.

The next morning, I receive a text from Will. He seems oblivious to any awkwardness at all and tells me he enjoyed the evening, which leaves me deeply confused.

"Anyways, it's a good thing you didn't come home with me, because I spent the night in the bathroom."

Apparently Will got violent food poisoning, which is strange because I was left unscathed by my meal. It strikes me as bizarre that this is the second time a man has become ill in my presence. Is this a coincidence, or fate keeping me away from the wrong men?

The property manager brings me a breakfast of black coffee, banana pancakes and slices of papaya. I wolf my food down before getting ready for another scuba dive. Putu collects me in an old pickup truck and drives to a nearby beach where a tiny boat is waiting. It's the width of a canoe, but much longer and has a set of outriggers along each side resembling two giant wings. We climb in and the captain cranks the engine, gliding the vessel across the waves to open water.

Putu and I put on our masks and fins before jumping in, vigorously treading while the captain hands down our floating BCD vests. It's a tricky maneuver. My right arm goes in with ease, but the other cannot find its respective hole, prompting my tight neck to spasm. I flounder in pain and thrash in the water, gasping for air after dunking under the surface. Putu glides over and assists my left arm into the hole before securing the clips like a parent helping their child into a life jacket.

I comfortably float and massage out the knot in my neck. We give each other a thumbs down and I release the air from my vest, equalizing my ears as my body sinks like a stone.

The Pyramids dive site is named after a set of iron rimmed boxes stacked on top of each other in a triangle shape. They are a host for coral transplants in a marine preservation project and it appears to be a success. The coral is thriving, and we see many different fish and sea creatures, including my personal favorite, the creepy moray eel.

We circumvent the pyramids and my 'monkey mind' begins to wander. While on one hand, I'm proud my dive skills are now advanced enough that I don't need 100% of my focus to remain safe, I'm dejected that even 20 meters below the ocean my thoughts are still out of control. One of the reasons I love diving so much is the absolute silence I feel; it's like jumping into a void where the past and future do not exist. It offers a direct connection to the present moment—or at least it did.

We begin our ascent to the surface and the visibility decreases from particles[18] floating in the water. Tiny pinpricks that sting and tingle radiate across my right shoulder. The sensation extends up the right side of my neck, into my ear and along my right jawline until suddenly, my lips are on fire!

I don't see jellyfish floating in the water, so I do not immediately know what is happening. My mind anxiously jumps to the worst-case scenario: I have the Bends. I imagine tiny nitrogen bubbles under my skin as the culprit of the burning sensation and fight off a wave of panic. I indicate to Putu with a thumbs up sign that I want to go up, and he responds by tapping the dive computer on his wrist: we have a three-minute safety stop, a measure implemented to prevent the Bends.

It's a long three minutes.

We ascend to the surface, and I struggle getting into the boat with the continued burning of my skin. Back at shore, I stumble off the boat and sprint like a maniac to the freshwater shower. Putu is still in the dark about what is

---

[18]In hindsight, I believe the particles were jellyfish stingers or jellyfish larvae known as sea lice.

happening and follows to ask if I'm okay.

"Ahh, jellyfish sting," he says nonchalantly, as if it happens all the time.

I'm not screaming or crying, so he must not realize the extent of my discomfort and doesn't help, though I'm not sure what he could do for me, other than urinate on my face. I'm not into that kind of thing.

Instead, I cancel my second dive.

"Oh, are you tired?"

My face is only melting off, no big deal.

"I'm in pain," I tell him gravely.

He assures me there is vinegar back at the dive shop which will neutralize the sting. We load up our gear into the truck and head out.

Back at the shop, I'm handed a roll of toilet paper and a bottle of white vinegar. I soak a wad and place it on my lower lip, which feels the size of a golf ball but only looks slightly more plump than usual. The acrid smell is enough to knock a bird clear from the sky, but I accept my fate of smelling like a fish and chips shop and dab the vinegar-soaked paper over my face.

I return to my guesthouse with only minor tingling, but by now, my health anxiety is the primary concern. Obsessive thoughts have taken hold: what if nitrogen bubbles are floating into my brain?

I spend the next hour on Google, researching diving

accidents and symptoms of the Bends before powering down my laptop for an early sleep.

I'm exhausted from my weekend of diving, which didn't go as smoothly as expected, provoking my anxiety rather than alleviating it. The exchange with Will was also unsettling, leaving me to wonder if I'm the common denominator to such uncomfortable encounters with men.

I swipe open my phone and hover over the dating app icon.

I press delete.

18

Less 'Rom' and more 'Com'

In case you haven't already guessed: this is not a love story.

If it were, I'd already be shacked up with TD&H (tall, dark and handsome), the French hunk I met standing outside a restaurant who prompted me to download the dating app in the first place. Our moment of 'waiting together, but not together', and our final parting glance as my taxi slowly pulled away would have been the 'meet cute' moment in our love story—if this memoir were a love story that is.

I never did meet the Frenchman again, nor the Italian I mistook for him on the dating app. If my life were a Rom-Com, TD&H's twin would have laughed over my mistake and playfully insinuated that I feigned the misrecognition as a smooth way to slide into his messages.

"Does that move actually work?" he'd ask, and I'd reply, "I don't know, did it?"

We'd tell this to a chuckling room of devoted guests at our Tuscan wedding before the crowd collectively clinks their champagne glasses, cuing a 'kiss the bride' moment—but that didn't happen either.

In my world, I'm the unintentional 'other woman' to an undercover movie star with a penchant for adultery and daddy dominatrix role play. The only thing 'falling' on one of my dates is a coconut shell onto my head. My longest romances are a 'situationship' with Cabernet Sauvignon and a fling with discounted airfare to far flung places.

Catch flights, not feelings.

I'm still a sucker for a good love story though; I particularly enjoy the cheesy Hallmark ones. In my favourite romance movie storyline, the big city career girl goes home for the holidays and ends up unexpectedly bumping into her high school sweetheart. He now owns a small business that's failing—usually a bookstore or a Christmas tree farm—and she just so happens to have the skills from her marketing job to save the day. They rekindle their old flame, save the business and find true love.

End scene.

Each December, I fly home to celebrate Christmas with my family in my hometown and the thought playfully sits in my mind. You see, I fit the Hallmark trope perfectly. The hopelessly single, thirty-something year old who left her small town behind in pursuit of something more: for me, that something is travel.

In real life though, I'd rather not run into an old flame while home for the holidays. It would be less of a rekindling, and more of a seismic alarm or bomb threat indicating impending disaster.

All systems on alert. Code black. I repeat. CODE BLACK!

In the movies, I've always wanted to know what happens next, after 'the happily ever after'. Does the big city career girl, who's clearly worked hard to get to where she is, give up the life she built brick by brick, and move back to her hometown for love?

I mean, maybe love is enough; it's perhaps the most important thing in life. Inevitably though, there's an unequal dynamic where she's sacrificing everything for love and he's not. She's giving something up and he's not. Is this really a dynamic that will lead to long-lasting love? Or will resentment inevitably rear its ugly head when reality sets in and she grapples with such huge changes to her identity and independence.

I want to believe in true love and that each of us will find our own happy ending, but I'm also realistic enough to know life doesn't always work out how we imagine. We have high expectations for a job, a relationship, a trip, a plan; but what happens when what we wanted so badly, ends up being what makes us unhappy?

I always imagined I would meet someone while traveling in a natural, organic way; our lifestyles would match, which would lead to co-creating a shared path forward. The truth is, I'm still building my life brick by brick, fluttering from one place to another. Even if I experienced success with the dating app, it would be complicated to figure out our next steps together when I need to figure that out for myself first.

…isn't that why I came to Bali in the first place?

19

The Digital Nomad Dream

They say home is where the heart is...but my heart is everywhere. The winding road never ceases. It twirls and curls and I follow on, packing and unpacking myself.

I've developed an uncanny ability to settle into places that aren't mine, creating a makeshift home wherever I go. The first thing you learn as a nomad working your way around the world, is that a travel lifestyle like this does not actually resemble a vacation. When you have a remote job that can be done from anywhere, it ends up just being 'everyday life' transplanted into a more desirable place, like tropical Bali instead of icy Canada.

I still run errands, go grocery shopping, cook myself meals and do my banking; what I've come to call life administration tasks that aren't as glamorous as working from beachfront cafes or trendy eateries.

Even then, I've never understood the digital nomads who post glorified content of themselves working by a pool. I tried it: the sun glares off the screen making it impossible to see and Wi-Fi can be an issue. Plus, I'm often preoccupied with people watching or disturbed by the many sights and sounds of a public space.

When I must buckle down and get work done, I confine myself to home. Day after day of this though, and suddenly my world feels quite small, void of any semblance of travel. The isolation is never a slow burn, gradually building day by day; it hits me suddenly, as if I never saw it coming. I'll realize I've slid back into the rut of my comfort zone, ironically the very thing I try to escape with my travel lifestyle.

I become an anxious homebody without her own home.

By this point, I've usually stuck around in one place long enough for the novelty to wear off and for my problems to finally catch up to me. The cracks inevitably appear; they always do one way, or another.

When everything is new and shiny, I'm buoyant and jovial—but eventually reality settles in—life is not always exciting and it's not a sustainable or a realistic expectation for it to be. It seems that my notion of what constitutes living life to the fullest is rooted within excitement, so I'm constantly pushing for bigger and better experiences that make me 'feel alive'.

When the dust settles after moving to a new place and I notice a glimmer of boredom or a wave of dissatisfaction, my impulse is to change my external environment. The thing is, the problem was never external; no matter how many times I move, it's still me who boards the plane and lands in the arrivals hall. The common denominator is me.

It's me, hi, I'm the problem. It's me.

The places and spaces I enter, and the people I engage with, are merely mirrors reflecting what is actually troubling me. Of course, it's easier to cast blame outwards; it subverts all personal accountability.

It doesn't matter where I'm temporarily living. I will land on the same question, over and over: "to what purpose does it serve for me to be here?" If I'm living the hermit life, working long hours holed up in a housesit, instead of making the most of being here, what's the point?

So, I'll move on to a new place and the cycle begins again.

Ironically, this constant changing of my external environment seems to be triggering the downfall of my mental health. It doesn't exactly bode well for the reinforcement of stable habits and routines. I gave up a long-term apartment in my hometown to move to Tanzania and conduct my doctoral research four years ago. I've been floating around ever since, primarily living out of a suitcase.

I'm starting to crave a home that I don't even have. It's not homesickness per se; strangely I've never felt homesick before. It's a longing for connection: to be tethered to a place and feel as if I belong somewhere.

The romantic side of me wants to believe that maybe for someone as nomadic as I, home is a special person. Yet dating is a challenge with a lifestyle that is inherently so temporary and transient. I want to form meaningful connections, but I don't stick around long enough to. I'm unrooted and sometimes it feels like unnecessary effort to try if I'm just going to leave…because deep down, I know that when faced with the decision to stay or go, I'm perpetually walking out the door.

It's a hard truth to swallow, that again and again, I choose to leave, but choosing to stay is like not choosing me; like surrendering to a version of myself that I don't want to return to. The old me no longer fits; I've expanded and outgrown her shell. Like a Matryoshka nesting doll, staying is like trying to force myself back into my old self.

Is this the human condition? To perpetually yearn for more?

I've never longed for material things, just a life positioned on the edge of ordinary. The desire to live an extraordinary life is both my rise and my downfall. It's led me to my greatest achievements, but from an egoic place of fear that without them, I won't matter. If I'm not constantly living life to the fullest in the most extreme of ways, like climbing mountains just to see the view from the top, then I'm not 'truly living'.

Life isn't the highs or the mountain tops though. It's the climb: a series of decisions and the ordinary moments in between. It's the grief and anger and horror, just as much as the mystery, magic and wonder.

I realize I'm ready to slow down and spread roots, so why don't I ever feel 'at home'?

A wet nose nudges against my chin and my eyes blink open. Neva nestles into my lap, her paws kneading my flesh like dough. Her claws occasionally snag my trousers and I'm acutely aware of her power to slice me. Instead, she grooms me like a mother cat: her bumpy tongue catches on the fabric like sandpaper on rough wood.

Something ricochets off the roof and her crescent moon pupils dilate to the size of dimes. Her tiny head tilts, listening. Before I can register what might have fallen, she's already gone. I follow suit and uncoil my legs, far less gracefully standing from my meditation cushion. It's only quarter after seven when I hear the slowing of a motorcycle outside the gate and brace myself for the coconut man.

Every other day, a Balinese neighbor delivers me two ginormous green coconuts. He even lobs off the tops with a machete and pours the nectar into a large jug for me. It saves me from copious plastic bottles of market bought coconut water and offers him a side hustle: win, win.

Except lately, the coconut man's visits are becoming progressively earlier. I'm often still in my pajamas with sleep-crusted eyes and hair jetting out at all angles when I hear from across the gate:

"Coco-nuuuutttttt."

The gate requires a key to open, but in such moments of urgency, like a man screaming coconut at the top of his lungs, I become frazzled and unable to remember where I've left my keys. When I manage to let him in, I realize I need to pay him and then it's a mad dash to find my wallet.

Due to our language barrier, I'm unable to negotiate an alternative arrangement than this, so I succumb to a coconut alarm clock. Somehow, google translate never crosses my mind and instead, I look to the bright side: at least he makes sure I'm out of bed early.

I resist the urge to scream when there is a second knock, a mere fifteen minutes later, cuing the same song and dance. This time it's the Balinese Grandmother of the family who owns the property, dressed in her ceremonial clothes. She smiles at me and gestures to the woven basket in her hands, containing several tiny offerings and incense sticks. Occasionally, she comes by to place offerings on the altar adjacent to the office. I smile and step aside so she can enter, and she elegantly glides down the concrete steps.

I'll take all the help I can get to cast away my demons, so I take a silent moment of gratitude for the extra offerings she leaves at the office doorway and on the kitchen counter. Like a ghost, she's gone before I can say goodbye.

I'm trying to adjust to a new routine that now involves part-time work analyzing data from a global health project in West Africa. I was already struggling to form and maintain meditation habits, so the sudden change in my schedule is like a juggling act.

The recent torrential rains have become my excuse to stay in and work from home, but it's a slippery slope to self-isolation. It's as if the rain serves as mother nature's permission slip for me to slow down and rest without the guilt trip that I 'should be doing more'. Such thoughts often quickly lead to existential dread where I become hyper-aware of my own mortality.

It's not that I think about dying; it's more of an awareness that each day we move one step closer to it. It pressurizes the notion of living life to the fullest, which subsequently makes me guilty about the times when I perceive that I'm not.

Intellectually, I know my value as a human being is more than my productivity. Yet I continually strive to 'do more' and to 'be more', never accepting that my life is good enough as it is, or that I'm good enough as I am.

The sunshine urges me out of the house.

By 8:00 o'clock, I lace up my trainers and force myself out the door, edging my scooter down the narrow path and through the village towards the center of town. Turning down a steep, pot-hole riddled laneway, I park at the entrance of the popular Campuhan Ridge Walk.

Despite the early hour, the trail is filled with two types of tourists: those clad in spandex, running or speed walking over the hilly ridge; and those dressed to the nines with a camera in tow. The former briskly dodge the latter, who frequently stop in the middle of the path to take photos.

A girl in a flowy white dress and wide brimmed hat stops and stands directly in front of me, blocking the trail to pose for her boyfriend's flashy camera. I'm forced off the path and onto the bushy shoulder to get around her. I increase my speed and pump my arms with vigor like an 80-year-old mall walker. It feels good to move my body and beads of sweat drip down the bridge of my nose and off my collarbone.

A family of five meander slowly, completely obstructing the path in a side-by-side pack formation. Rather than crawl through a bush to get around them, I call from behind:

'Excuse me!"

They turn around and completely stop. Expressions of surprise mark their faces, as if they'd never expected someone else might wish to pass by. One of them steps aside for me to continue, before resuming their quintuple formation.

I shake my head and roll my eyes in frustration.

Spending time in public places, particularly those with

crowds, often leaves me drained and dejected. My chronic over-thinking prompts me to constantly consider the needs and comforts of those around me, even if they are complete strangers. When this same level of thoughtful consideration is inevitably not returned, such as with something as simple as blocking a public walking path, I often feel small and invisible, or self-righteous and resentful. Today it's the latter, which validates my recent hermit preferences.

Reaching the end of the ridge, I turn back the way I came, picking up even more speed. I'm eager for a coffee as a reward for exercising; I see it in my mind's eye like a carrot dangling in front of my face.

I pop into Cafe Vespa, stowing my laptop in my bag in case a moment of brilliance strikes. It's surprisingly empty, with patrons perhaps hunkering down at home to avoid the rain, which could be imminent judging by the dark sky. I order an oat milk latte and settle into a corner table, opening my laptop.

The side wall of the cafe has a cut out, revealing a man pacing back and forth while talking on his phone. There is loud, spa-like music on two speakers and clanking in the kitchen. Pacing cell phone guy is now smoking and the cigarette fumes billow into the cafe. My right leg jiggles like a jack hammer and I re-read the same sentence on my screen over and over. A tiny pulse of frustration ripples through me.

I don't know why I even try to work in public spaces. I can't focus unless I lock myself in a quiet room at home, but the monotony and isolation are giving me cabin fever.

It's as if my body doesn't filter sounds out as insignificant background noise. Instead, I'm aware of each sound individually and all at once. It incites panic and my tummy flips, like the moment a roller coaster barrels down a steep track. Days like today, I'm no longer in control of my mind.

I'm reading about the science behind spiritual awakenings and learn MRIs show the neural pathways active during awakenings are the same as those active during depression. The latter have decreased activity in the prefrontal cortex, while people consistently engaging in spiritual practices have increased activity in this same area.

What happens for someone who falls into both camps? I'm yo-yoing from one extreme to the other.

On a good day I feel saintly, emanating a warm smile and genuine glow as I interact with others. The next day, I'll avoid eye contact and conversation all together, retreating into my own inner world.

Naturally, this projects a 'hot and cold' demeanor with ever-fluxing moods and energy levels that even I struggle to understand.

Don't get me wrong. I'm quite fortunate that my inner

voice is supportive and encouraging, with dialogue like, "Come on Steph, just a little further! You can do it, one foot in front of the other."

Except, it's not like I'm running a marathon. I'm just trying to complete a few meager hours of mediocre work and remember to feed myself.

Two ladies enter the empty cafe and sit across from one another at the narrow table directly beside me. This phenomenon has always baffled me. If the entire space is open and free, why sit as close as possible to the only other person? Don't others also enjoy personal space and privacy? Or do they instinctively gravitate to people like magnets, assuming the best places are those already staked out?

One of the ladies has a jarringly loud voice, accentuated by the absence of other patrons, and it layers onto the other noises that haven't faded into the background. I'm not intentionally eavesdropping, but I'm incapable of not hearing their conversation.

Just as I'm debating whether to move tables, she confides in her friend:

"I'm often told that I'm too loud…I'm 'too much' for people. It used to make me really self-conscious, like I couldn't be myself."

I never considered loud people might not be comfortable occupying the space they seem to so easily 'take up'. As an anxious person, I struggle with taking up space in a different way, playing small to avoid conflict, while simultaneously sacrificing my wants and needs. I'm flooded with compassion and shame for judging this stranger. It seems our struggles are the same at their core:

'I'm too much' is just another expression of 'I'm not enough'.

20

Sink or Swim

Ana has returned to Bali and invites me to join her for a yoga class at a small studio in the center of Ubud. We take her grey Honda scoopy and I ride on the back as she expertly drives us down the narrow concrete track and through traffic to the studio.

Before class, we meet the owner, a beautiful European woman with long, soft waves despite the humidity. She's wearing a stylish wide-brimmed hat, a crochet bralette and high waisted yoga pants. Her hands glitter with delicate gold-plated rings, some adorned with chunky crystals, and I notice a matching gold armband on her toned bicep. She gestures to the wall behind us, stocked with white linen pieces and matching yoga sets, and informs us the pants she's modeling are a new addition to her clothing line.

We climb the stairs to the loft space and claim two spots at the front. The owner sets up a harmonium and begins the class by guiding us through a seated meditation. We sit cross-legged with eyes closed and she serenades us, crooning about Lord Ganesha the remover of obstacles.

The owner leads us through a dynamic vinyasa style class, flowing from plank to upward dog and back to downward dog. The room is exceedingly hot, and I find myself taking frequent breaks to guzzle water or rest in child's pose. I'm grateful for the end of the 90-minute sequence.

After class, Ana and I sit in the in-house café, chatting over coffee. The owner approaches us to say goodbye, before leaving hand-in-hand with Chad, the eccentric jumping teacher from Yoga Barn.

That checks out.

Ana has plans to spend the weekend in Bali and highly recommends I visit Sideman, a gorgeous village towards the East of the island.

She will need her scooter this weekend, so I've come to yoga with my bag packed and order a Gojek to take me straight to the Green Vanilla Farm in Sideman. The property has several cabins with private terraces overlooking sweeping views of a neighboring, multi-leveled rice field. I even have my own swing set facing the paddies.

What I failed to realize when reserving my cabin, is the farm's location. It's a solid twenty minutes outside of

Sideman. My Gojek app does not appear to work here, so I'm forced to ask my hosts about a bike rental to get around.

They have one left. I walk out front to the parking area and am surprised to see a sporty N-Max motorbike. Immediately, I think of Keeran's bandaged leg and tiny Vlad teetering away from the scene of the accident after he crashed into my scooter. My heart dances in my chest with nervous anticipation. Am I ready to drive this?

It's time to sink or swim.

The bike handles similar to Ana's Honda scoopy, but with a lot more power. I gingerly edge down the driveway and turn left onto a back road to practice until I'm sufficiently satisfied I'm in control of the beast—that is, until I reach my first hairpin turn. The road coils up and down the hillside in sharp turns on steep angles far too close to vertical for my liking. I'm nervous and drive at a snail's pace, causing the estimated twenty-minutes to double.

I cruise by Balinese ladies laying rice across tarps to dry in the sun. One tarp completely covers the road, and I slow, wondering what the etiquette is. Do I just drive over it? I edge along the left side and moments later, discover I'm back in the same place, approaching the same obstructive tarp.

Surely, I did not just drive in a circle?

I continue down the road and notice a hotel sign that I recognize from earlier and pull over to check my map. I'd taken a wrong turn on a winding, spindly back road, driving in a complete circle. I find my way back to the main road, which turns out to be much easier to drive.

An open-air café directly opposite a rice field catches my attention and I pull over and park. Settling into a bean bag cushion in front of a low coffee table, I order a tropical smoothie bowl. I'm sitting at the farthest table beside the restrooms, and a calico cat dozing beside me like a furry cherub attracts attention from patrons on their way to the porcelain throne.

I'm wearing my noise canceling headphones and don't notice a woman approach me, so I suddenly jump out of my skin when she begins to stomp her feet. She's excited to see the cat and jumps up and down while clapping her hands. Peering over me to look at the cat, she's too close for comfort. I hold my breath, keeping my gaze down.

Somehow, it never occurs to me to greet the woman and shift aside so she can easily meet the cat. Instead, I'm thrown off and instinctively tense up, avoiding her eye contact. When I glance back to her stomping grounds from my peripheral vision, she's gone. The cat continues to doze, unaware of its popularity.

Returning to my motorbike before the sun begins to dip in the sky, I make my way back to the farm. On one particularly steep incline, the bike shudders and struggles to climb the hill, suddenly stalling. I turn the engine off and back on, attempting to restart the engine, but nothing happens.

The bike is automatic, so I'm both confused and nervous. I try again with the same result.

Shit.

I'm stalled at the top of a hill which immediately winds into a blind hairpin turn. I quickly realize the danger of this situation; oncoming traffic could whip around at any second and careen into me. I can't simply walk the bike to the shoulder of the road though. I'm on such a steep angle that I'm fighting gravity to keep the heavy bike upright. Moving to the shoulder would mean laying it down on its side.

Just as I'm mentally debating what to do, an angel on Earth approaches. A Balinese man on a scooter climbs the hill from behind me and notices my distress. Without a word of English, he parks his bike on the shoulder and pantomimes for me to get off, while he steadies the handlebars and proceeds to climb on. The bike starts on his first try. He drives it to the top of the hill past the blind corner and parks on flat ground. I'm mortified but there's no time for ego. I'm still standing at the top of the hill at the blind corner. I run up to him and he hands me back the keys.

"Terima kasih!" I say with gratitude.

Without a single word, he walks down the hill to his parked bike and drives off. Trying again to start the engine, the bike starts with ease. I exhale a heavy sigh of relief and immediately drive back to the farm to turn in the rental, knowing with certainty I won't be driving it again.

21

Health and Happiness…
Or Something like that

Back in Ubud, I meet De, a Balinese high priestess offering spiritually inclined tourists healing experiences.

She tells me before the pandemic, she operated a yoga studio in a popular area in Ubud near Monkey Forest but was forced to close her business when tourism dried up. Now she works one-on-one with tourists offering private day tours, like mountain top yoga, trips to Mt. Batur and cleansing ceremonies at Balinese temples.

De takes me to a nearby water temple for a ritual steeped in ancestral knowledge and tradition. Melukat is believed to clean and purify the body, mind and spirit from our present and past lives, fostering healing and vitality. De has come prepared with an orange sarong for me, which she helps me tie over my bathing suit like a halter-top dress, before changing into her own white robes.

She adopts a more serious demeanor, leading me to the altar area adjacent to the water temple. I'm instructed to sit cross-legged with my eyes closed for a brief meditation, while De lights an incense stick. She places canang sari, a Balinese offering in front of me and says a prayer in Bahasa. De instructs me to place the offering on the altar before leading me to the water.

We descend several concrete steps into a small pool of cold water that reaches our chests. Five oval shaped fountains are mounted above the pool and forcefully spout water towards us, causing me to lose my footing. De must be used to this, as she stands strong. She offers me an arm as if helping an elderly person and I clutch onto her for balance.

We start at the first fountain on the left and I'm instructed to think of my body being cleansed while De places my head under the water. I nearly panic after running out of breath and come up gasping, not realizing there's a pocket of air beyond the flow of water. She smiles reassuringly, placing a hand on my back for support and I try again. This time, holding onto the fountain with my hands, I allow the water to flow over my head and down my back.

We move right to the next fountain, where I cleanse my mind. The next three fountains are for my heart, soul and finally my karma, at which point I notice a small bird has landed on top of the fountain. I take this to be a good omen.

After the purification ritual, I'm exuberant, light and joyful. Imagine bottling up the essence of how it feels to have sunshine on your face; to laugh until your belly hurts, to receive an unexpected act of kindness; to smell the earth after it rains; or to hug a cherished loved one. Imagine it's possible to combine these things and spray it over yourself like a mist, allowing the energy to absorb into your skin.

That is how I felt after being cleansed.

The only experience that has come close to this was my two months on Kythnos, the Greek island I lived on during one of the lockdowns. I was staying there temporarily, building my virtual yoga studio and felt deeply inspired by the abundant beauty around me.

Meditation no longer felt difficult; it was a natural part of my routine. I spent the mornings deep in creative work that I adored and the afternoons sunbathing on a deserted beach entirely to myself. There was hardly anyone coming and going due to travel restrictions, so my two-months were spent in complete isolation, aside from weekly grocery deliveries and a local tour guide I met. I was far from lonely, lapping up solitude like sweet cream, suspended in joy and peace.

During this time, I felt no emotions typically associated as 'negative'. It was as if I was looking at everything from the top of a mountain, so far removed from worries and anxieties that they became insignificant.

Stress about money? *I have everything I need.* Apprehension of my business failing? *What's meant to be, will be.* Fear of what others think? *What they think doesn't affect me.* Insecurities about my appearance? *I am more than my body.* Uncertainty of the future? *I'm exactly where I need to be now.* Societal pressures of finding love? *I am the love that I seek.*

Friends and family members noticed and commented on the difference in my demeanor, admitting that maybe there really is something to this meditation thing after all. One morning, while sitting in the sunshine on my terrace overlooking the Aegean Sea, I had a sobering epiphany.

Of course I didn't have any negative feelings; how could I, when I had virtually zero triggers? I was living like a monk in complete isolation in paradise. There were no people around me to test this new neutrality I'd found: no one to make noise that would typically fluster me, and no one to behave in ways I might have taken personally or passed judgement on.

While I was undoubtedly thriving in my personal relationships, they were still long-distance relationships; I could engage as much, or as little, as I wanted by simply turning on or off my phone.

It was like I had found the volume dial for life and placed it on mute. My other senses became stronger, and everything felt lighter and brighter. Yet, I questioned the sustainability of my new-found peace in 'in the real world' beyond the protective bubble of the island.

With rumors of the ferry back to Athens shutting down, I knew it was time to return to mainland. Within mere days, I fell from grace and reunited with anxiety and depression, almost as fast as a light flicking from on to off.

Hello darkness, my old friend.[19]

After my purification ceremony with De, I embody a glimmer of the buoyant light I exuded in Greece. For a few short hours, it's as if all my pain, worries, fears, grievances, and struggles were washed away in the water.

Perhaps this is simply a result of spending the day with De—who has one of the most pure, warm energies I have

---

[19]I still grapple with the spiritual face-plant I experienced in Athens. On Kythnos, it felt like I tapped into something universal. It felt so good, my instinct was to protect it. I wanted to continue feeling good, so I avoided anything that might make me feel bad: until suddenly I realized my world had become quite small. I was literally 'alone on a deserted island' and it wasn't as if I could stay there forever. I unintentionally used my spiritual practices as escapism, to entirely avoid the emotions and relationship dynamics that were challenging for me. Rather than facing this inner work, I completely bypassed it in pursuit of positivity. Eventually the emotions I thought I'd transcended, resurfaced with a vengeance.

ever encountered—or the Balinese water temple truly cleansed what needed to be rinsed away.

What I do know with certainty, is the effect disappeared by the next morning. I returned to mere human status, inflicted by a vicious cycle of manic thoughts and dense emotions.

22

Peace, Love, and Nasi Goreng

The Gilis are a trio of islands—Gili Trawangan, Gili Meno and Gili Air—off the west coast of Lombok. They are a popular detour for travelers in Bali, known for white sand beaches, coral reefs and stunning turquoise waters.

Ana is back in Bali for a week, so I book a last-minute ferry ticket to the Gilis. I've heard tales of harrowing journeys on tiny speed boats toppling over huge waves, where passengers crammed like sardines in a can, feared for their lives or were too seasick to care. Ekyjaya is a much larger vessel with upper deck seating and I'm willing to pay more to avoid living out a horror story. I reserve a ticket on the 9:00am ferry.

Padangbai, the port village where the boat departs, is an hour from Ubud by motorbike. I order a Gojek shortly after 7:00am and walk down to the village to meet the driver. He cancels the ride, so I order a second driver and get a latte from Ubud Coffee Roastery while I wait.

By now, it's been 45 minutes and I'm still waiting with a flip in my stomach, worrying about missing the boat. My driver finally arrives, and I pop in earbuds to listen to an audiobook on the ride, which is quite pleasant in the cool morning air. When we reach Padangbai, we're halted by a ceremonial procession. It's now 8:55am and I'm skeptical I'll make the boat.

Suddenly an elderly man in white ceremonial clothes, with three grains of white rice on his third eye directs me onto the back of his motorcycle. He says he's driving by the Ekyjaya office and will drop me there. I palm the Gojek driver cash for the fare and hop on the back of the stranger's bike.

It turns out the office is less than a block away. I could have walked but given my rush to make the boat, I'm grateful for the lift. I hop off and thank him before rushing towards the reception desk.

"Where you going miss?"

"Gili Air."

He hands me a rectangular sticker with the island name printed on it, which I place on my chest like a name tag.

I've made it just in time!

The other stragglers and I are directed down a sandy pathway to the harbor where the boat is waiting. I feel like a late passenger who's held up an aircraft, but no one seems to notice.

The boat is much bigger than I expected and even still, there are few seats left. I climb up to the top deck, which has metal benches loaded with passengers and luggage. There is one remaining, partially obstructed by a suitcase I'm now using as a backrest. Taking in the sun on my face and wind in my hair, I'm elated.

Our first stop is Gili Trawangan where a swarm of at least 300 travelers wait on the dock. They clumsily clamber around with wheeled bags, resembling hurried ants in a busy colony. We dock and the crowd surges forward, desperate to get out of the sun and on their way. I'm enormously relieved to not be in that line!

We drop off passengers bound for Gili T. and pick up those headed back to Bali before continuing to Gili Meno. When we finally approach the third and final island, Gili Air, the crew corrals disembarking passengers like sheep. A water taxi approaches to shuttle us into the tiny harbor, hovering beside our vessel. I cautiously step on board and stand, holding onto an overhead rail like riding a subway car.

The island is small, a mere five square kilometers, and there are no cars or motorbikes. Compared to the hustle and bustle of Ubud, with dense traffic and copious honking, Gili Air feels eerily empty and silent.

I immediately love it.

My guesthouse is only a few blocks from the ferry, so I walk. The main road in the centre of the island dissects the land in two halves, and I head north. I pass the trendy 'Barefoot Blondie' cafe, several dress shops, a vegan restaurant and a bookstore before finding an alley to the property. There are at least eight bungalows of varying sizes, each with its own terrace and hammock.

I take a cold shower and change into my bathing suit, a creamsicle colored two-piece, and walk to the beach. The tide is out so I wade through ankle deep water, dodging sharp shells and spiky pieces of bleached coral. Eventually, sinking backwards into water that's as warm as a bathtub, I float on my back, immensely gratified. Something about the ocean is healing, as if the saltwater cleanses all my worries away.

The next morning, I meet my neighbor in the guesthouse communal area during breakfast. We chat over coffee and banana pancakes and Dan tells me he's a semi-retired American from Portland. He's not much bigger than me, with an athletic but slight frame and a brown military-grade crew cut. Our conversation is casual, so I don't think twice when he mentions the same plan as me to bicycle around the island.

Dan 'coincidentally' leaves at the same time as I do. We both ride counterclockwise and continually bump into each other along the beachfront path. The road quickly dissipates into dense sand, causing my bike to lurch forward to a sudden stop. I'm content moving at a slow pace and walk alongside my bike through the sand, while Dan disappears ahead.

I'm dripping with sweat and abandon my bike at a beachside bar called 'Legends'. Claiming a table with two bean bag chairs facing the turquoise water, I sit under a wide umbrella, reading a book and sipping on cinnamon coffee with coconut cream.

I jump when Dan suddenly appears over my shoulder, red-faced and perspiring heavily. He tells me he made it entirely around the island and is desperate to cool off in the water, so he's going to snorkel out to the reef.

"I can watch your bag if you want," I offer.

…and the saga begins.

When he returns from the water, Dan sinks into the unoccupied bean bag chair. He yammers on about his snorkeling expedition, emanating a modern-day Robinson Crusoe, proudly boasting about whittling a stick down to a pointy spear to catch fish "with his bare hands".

"Ohhh…cool. Did you catch anything?"

"No…"

Apparently, he'd met a British lady earlier who's also traveling solo, and she meanders over from the bar next door to say hi. I'm grateful for her presence, which seems to dilute any concerns Dan intentionally found me at Legends. We all plan to meet up later as a trio for sunset and she suggests 'The Cheeky Monkey', a popular bar on the West side of the island.

Later, we sit on rainbow-colored cushions swapping travel stories and watching the sun dip below the horizon. The British lady is catching the early morning ferry and wants to return to her hotel early. Dan and I walk our bikes alongside her to make sure she gets home safe, before riding back to our guesthouse at a mere 8:30pm. I don't mind; I'm utterly exhausted from the sun, sand and socialization and take the opportunity to have an early sleep.

The call to prayer wakes me at 4:45am. I've planned to attend a yoga class at 'Flowers and Fire' at the suggestion of a fellow travel blogger who's currently based here in Gili Air working remotely.

"It would be lovely to see you," she writes in an Instagram message inviting me to the class.

I walk to breakfast, secretly hoping American Dan has already taken his. I'm tired and not in the mood to hang out with him today. On cue, almost as if he'd been waiting for my entrance to the common area, he rushes over and sits beside me.

Now, without caffeine, I'm limited in all-around alertness and mental acuity, so pleasant small talk is arduous.

"My back got so fried snorkeling yesterday."

He proceeds to tell me about his sunburn and set of blistered toes from ill-fitting flippers, leaning forward to slide his shirt up to show me his back. I'm grateful he exercises self-restraint and doesn't show me his feet—I don't care to see a strange man's blistered toes, especially while eating.

"It's gonna peel so bad, I've got to find some aloe vera today."

I suggest coconut oil as a substitute, to which he responds that since he can't reach his back very well and therefore can't keep it clean, he worries about clogged pores and 'backne'.

I'm still half asleep. My severe caffeine addiction means I need at least two cups before I'm fully alert. I merely wish to sip my coffee in peace without conversation, let alone discussions of impending blemishes on the trapezius of a man I barley know (and rather wish not to know right about now).

"So, what are you up to today, Steph?"

I mention my plan to meet a friend at yoga this morning and without hesitation, he invites himself to join. It's not a private catch-up or exclusive event, so I don't mind that he comes along, but I'm mildly concerned by how easily he interjects himself into my plans.

Dan and I walk to the yoga studio together at 8:00am and I briefly check my phone on the Wi-Fi when we arrive. I have a message from my blogger friend: she can't make it. Without another person to dilute the one-on-one dynamic with Dan, I'm starting to feel like I'm on a date I didn't agree to.

We claim spots at the front in the open-air loft studio and unroll our mats for a 90-minute vinyasa class, taught by a petite blonde American in her early twenties.

Afterwards, I tell Dan I want to get some writing done.

"I'm going to stick around for a coffee here, I brought my journal."

"Ohhh great idea! I could use a cup of coffee."

He plunks down on a large couch and pulls out his phone to connect to the Wi-Fi.

Solo travel normally offers a wide degree of control for how much or how little socialization you want on a trip. It's easy to meet other travelers, and it's (usually) easy to duck off somewhere alone with a book or laptop. This is the first time in nearly ten years of travel where I'm having difficulty establishing my own time and space when I want it.

Dan drones on about his upcoming travel plans, wavering between two destinations and asking for advice to alleviate his indecisiveness. I'm unable to journal and listen simultaneously, and stow my notebook back in my tote bag, resigning to chit chat.

Eventually I excuse myself, blaming the noise of the coffee shop and citing my desire to write elsewhere. Thankfully he takes my hint and doesn't leave with me. I walk home feeling overstimulated; my long hair whips around like a halo of medusa coils orbiting my head and the flowing dress I changed into after yoga billows up in the strong breeze.

An ocean dip might calm my nerves but judging by the fierce waves and lack of swimmers, it might feel more like a washing machine rinse cycle. I take a cold shower at the guesthouse and change into comfier clothes, returning to my hammock.

Hours later, I'm still lounging in my hammock reading a book when Dan appears beside my terrace, smiling mischievously.

"Yo, wanna smoke some ganja?"

Did he just say yo?

He casually slides his hand out of his board shorts, revealing a leafy parcel in his palm. He tells me he procured

'Mary Jane' (his words, not mine) from the bungalow owner, an Indonesian man with long shaggy hair who I noticed staring into space with glossy eyes; the latter detail now begins to make more sense.

Dan giggles.

Jeez, he's higher than a kite.

He pauses, looking as if there's something more he wants to say.

"By the way, I told the owner we hung out last night and um…I think maybe things were lost in translation. Just so you know, in case anything is weird with him."

I think back to hours earlier when I walked past the owner. He looked at me as if he knew a wicked secret about me. I imagine it's the same kind of expression he'd have if he spotted me on a walk of shame from Dan's bungalow after a roll in the sack.

I didn't know why he looked at me like this at the time, but now I'm certain it was not my imagination. I read between the lines that Dan generously exaggerated our 'hang out' to the owner, insinuating something transpired between us.

I'm incredibly annoyed.

Did I give him a wrong impression?

I silently think back to the series of events over the last few days; but with resounding certainty, I know my only 'infraction' was being too friendly to a lonely, middle-aged man at breakfast.

Dan is still standing there, subtly swaying on his feet and looking at me with googly eyes, suggesting the 'ganja' has now reached his brain cells—brain cells which I imagine are valiantly fighting for their lives. Otherwise, why on earth would he admit he talked about me to the owner?

It's weird and I'm profusely uncomfortable.

"Okay.... Anyways, I'm going to get back to reading now. Safe travels tomorrow if I don't see you."

Dan is taking off tomorrow morning and I hope my dismissal seals off any thoughts he might have of another hang out on his last night, ganja related or not.

My recent antisocial behavior is again justified. I'm increasingly resigned to believe it's just easier and often more comfortable to be alone, than dodge unwanted encounters like this. Plus, if I experience something wonderful on my own, there are no awkward moments or contentious characters to 'taint' the memory: it's mine, and mine alone to cherish.

My blogger pal invites me to dinner with some of her friends. I meet the group at 'Alora', an open-air Italian restaurant illuminated by twinkling fairy lights. The group orders glasses of Malbec to accompany appetizers, and I'm surprised how easily I relinquish my sobriety, justifying a glass of wine as a treat.

The first sip alters my brain chemistry. I'm buoyant, as if floating on my back in the salty, turquoise water. The wine is like sandpaper, softening the edges of my thoughts.

Drinking comes as easy as trying on an old pair of shoes molded to my feet: it's familiar and comfortable. I'm simultaneously aware this wouldn't be happening if I was dining alone, but it's not like I felt peer pressure to drink; the group meal is more of an excuse to.

The problem is, I never have just one.

Our food comes out and the group orders a bottle to share. An Australian guy takes the lead, topping up everyone's glass. I graze on vegetarian ravioli with truffle oil and savor the rich, smoky taste of the wine on my tongue while trying to pace myself with everyone else's slower sips.

After our meal, someone suggests we head to the Barefoot Blondie for cocktails. The upstairs is packed with mingling travellers and expats alike, huddled together and chatting over bass-blasting music. A chalk board behind the bar shows an array of creative cocktails on offer, like 'You're One in a Melon'. I join the dinner crew at the bar and order a 'too hot to handle' Margarita with fresh pineapple and jalapeno. We dramatically toast each other, clinking glasses and sipping with theatrics.

I'm joined by a much younger European guy who leans on the bar and tells me he's passing through the Gilis before traveling onwards to Komodo island. I take a final sip of my cocktail, before sharing that I'm living in Bali and am just here for the week.

He asks if I'd like another, and I nod nonchalantly. Waving over the bartender, he orders two more, paying with a fistful of bills. I thank him and we clink cocktail glasses, at which point he reminds me it's important to maintain eye contact while sipping after a toast, or it can bring bad luck. "Seven years of bad sex," he clarifies with a wink.

I internally cringe at the line I've heard too many times to count, but go along with it for the plot, staring into his brown eyes as I sip. His friend calls him over to a corner booth and I push through the undulating crowd to the edge of the bar, where my dinner companions have since claimed a table. A petite blonde twerks on the bar, and I recognize her as my yoga teacher from the other morning.

I guzzle down two more cocktails before we close the bar, and spill into the street. Drunk and barefoot travellers are fired up, discussing an after party. The dinner crew decides to continue onwards to Legends, the same beachside bar where the Dan saga began. I'm now at least six drinks deep and tipsy on my feet after so many months without a drop of alcohol and instead, decide to put myself to bed.

I loosely planned to island hop over to Lombok on the 7:45am public ferry the next morning, but now have a strong sense this won't be happening. I had a fun night, but simultaneously feel guilty for throwing away five months of sobriety without so much as a second thought.

23

No Worry, Chicken Curry

I wake up again at the call to prayer from the neighborhood mosque and guzzle an entire liter of water before collapsing horizontally. By 8:00am, I cautiously sit up on the edge of the bed. I have a slight headache, but nothing a couple of ibuprofens and a coffee can't fix.

At the common area over breakfast, I re-evaluate my travel plans, enormously grateful American Dan is no longer here to yap at me. Over the years, my travel planning has become extremely lax. I'd like to say this is due to my free-spirited and relaxed personality which 'goes with the flow', but I'm just disorganized.

This has a negative side to it of course: I'm often forced to pay more when booking last minute or find sold-out hotels for my travel dates. Traveling without a plan has its advantages though. I personally find even the best laid out plans never unfold as expected. There can be interruptions to travel after getting sick, or in my case, a hangover. It's easy to alter or adjust an itinerary when nothing was booked in the first place. In this way, there's flexibility to stay longer in a destination I've come to love, or to move on faster than anticipated from one which doesn't resonate.

I decide I'm in no state to navigate Lombok on a rental scooter and make the split decision to island hop over to Gili Trawangan for my remaining nights. I use the guesthouse Wi-Fi to book a budget hotel and return to my room to pack up. I don't know the boat schedule and don't want to ask the guesthouse owner, whom I'm now creeped out by (thanks Dan).

I'll wing it.

After checking out, I walk to the harbor, passing the Barefoot Blondie and silently fighting off a wave of nausea in memory of the cocktails consumed there. I soldier on to the docks and find there's a water taxi about to depart. I pay for a ticket before hustling over to the boat filled with waiting travellers.

Younger backpackers look to be in a similar rocky state, clutching bottles of water and oversized packs at their feet. An older couple clad in fanny packs and velcro Teva sandals rub suncream on each other's shoulders. Another solo female clocks me, and we exchange smiles as I sit across from her. She gets off at the next stop: Gili Meno.

When we reach Gili Trawangan, I'm relieved as we approach an empty stretch of sand and not the chaotic dock I witnessed days prior with a crowd of 300 travellers. I remove my flip-flops and roll up my pants before climbing down the back of the boat into knee deep water.

My guesthouse is a mere five-minute walk down the main road, which is packed with tourists on bicycles and horse drawn buggies carting around new arrivals and their luggage. The salty air smells of musky horse and manure; the latter is sprinkled under a line of buggies waiting for passengers like a que of taxis at an airport.

I turn left onto a cobblestone alley towards a less busy road and find my guesthouse. It's more of a motel with two strips of side-by-side rooms facing an interior garden. I'm unable to check in before 2:00pm, so I leave my bag behind the front desk and take off on a rental bicycle.

Compared to Gili Air, the streets here are either paved or packed down dirt paths, and it's much easier to navigate by bike. I cycle around the entire island over the next hour, profusely sweating off my hangover.

Beach boys slinging drinks behind tiki bars blasting Reggae music call to me as I cycle by, "Mushrooms Miss?"

I notice a sign advertising Mushroom Milkshakes with 'magic levels' ranging from low to 'fucking bloody sexy'. Drugs are highly illegal in Indonesia and there are well known cases of ignorant and non-complaint tourists facing jail time. Possession charges depend on the type and quantity of drug, with the strictest punishments being life in prison or execution[20]. It's a roll of the dice I'm not willing to gamble.

"No thank you!" I call back as I bike by.

"Hakuna Matata, No worries."

I'm momentarily nostalgic for my time living in Tanzania, and chuckle at hearing a Kiswahili phrase on a tiny Indonesian island in the Indian Ocean. Hakuna Matata does literally translate into English as 'no worries', as the Lion King song suggests.

I stop at another beachfront cafe not peddling magic mushrooms and bop along to a local rendition of 'Land Down Under' by Men at Work on a nearby speaker:

"We come from Gili Meno, Magic Mushroom for breakfast, sometimes. Don't come to Gili Meno, if you're scared of mosquitos."

I claim an empty sunbed and ask for a menu. I've missed lunch and I'm ravenous, but incompetent of making up my mind. Frankly, I'm preoccupied with whether to order a cold

---

[20]At the time of writing this book in 2024, a "drug lab" in Canggu was raided by police, leading to the arrest of several Russian and Ukrainian expats. Police estimate the enterprise pocketed a quarter of a million US dollars while operating out of a villa, prompting some community members to call for the harshest punishment: execution. It's unclear at this time whether they will join Indonesian inmates on death row or receive a lighter sentence. However, past drug charges laid on tourists have led to in-country imprisonment, suggesting Indonesia does not offer leniency to guilty foreigners.

beer. My alcohol binge has opened the floodgates to casual drinking. Before, I was determined to take a hiatus from alcohol on my extended stay in Bali in the name of health, so drinking didn't occupy my mind. I mentally compartmentalized it away as not being a possibility in the same way I do with abstaining from meat as a vegetarian. Now I justify it easily because I've already 'ruined' my sobriety, so why not?

A gecko hiding in the rafters of the beach umbrella I'm sitting under, suddenly shits. Brownish green speckles rain down directly onto the menu I'm holding, as if to say, "shit or get off the pot miss". That explains the uncanny number of flies vehemently buzzing around my sunbed. I'm too tired and lazy to move. I hand the defecated menu back to my smiling server, who seems oblivious to the flies, or just entirely unphased.

"One cold Bintang please."

"No worry, chicken curry."

He flashes me a hang loose 'shaka' sign with his hand like a surfer and I laugh in return at this unexpected one-liner. He brings me an ice-cold beer and I happily ignore the fly on my foot, taking a long pull from the icy bottle. A generous heap of Nasi Goreng comes next, and I shovel it down between sips of lager, while admiring the calm turquoise water.

The next morning, I sign up for a snorkel trip to Gili Meno. I'm worried my recent resurgence of anxiety would follow me into the depths if I were to go scuba diving, and don't want to risk underwater panic. Besides, a boat trip sounds fun!

I wear denim shorts over my orange bikini and meet my tour guide near the harbor at 9:00am sharp. We board a small fishing boat and glide over the waves towards the neighboring island. I'm given a mask with a snorkel and fins, which I make sure fit my feet correctly to avoid blistered toes.

We anchor at our first stop: an underwater statue riddled with floundering tourists circling the attraction like sharks around a bucket of chum. Some violently thrash their limbs, while others remain vertical at the surface, treading water like bobbing buoys. I'm unable to occupy space without someone doggy paddling into me with long, scratching nails. I hover out of the way to regroup, and a man surfaces directly underneath me, unintentionally head-butting my—well, my butt.

I return to the boat, overwhelmed by the swarm of snorkellers. The captain navigates our boat away from the crowd and we plunge into vacant waters, immediately spotting a ginormous turtle. It elegantly glides through the water, occasionally popping to the surface for air before diving back down. We follow from a distance, before turning to observe fish populating a coral reef. In the absence of motorboats, I hear the familiar crackling noise of living coral, reminiscent of pop rocks candy.

My guide and I climb back into the boat and approach Gili Meno for a break on land. I hop off the boat, eagerly wading towards the pristine white sand beach. I claim a lounge chair and order an iced coffee, opening the book I brought. There are no umbrellas for shade, but I'm content dipping in the water to cool off.

I only peg my rookie mistake when we return to the boat, and I sit on the hard bench inside the vessel. I notice a familiar tightening of the skin on my back and bottom, as if it shrunk one-size too small. Swiveling around, I attempt to look at my lower back and notice a fuchsia colour.

Uh-oh.

In my experience, the full extent of a sunburn is only known after getting out of the sun and taking a shower, so I know it's bad if the burn is this visible at this stage. We head back to Gili T. and I race home to my room for a shower, which seals my lobster fate. The entire back half of my body is scorched from floating on the surface to snorkel, including my bottom. A tan line is strikingly etched on my red behind, resembling white bikini bottoms. I take my own advice and slather coconut oil generously over my warm skin.

I succumb to a motionless last night on my belly under the air conditioner. While my trip to the Gili islands did not turn out how I imagined, inclusive of a stage-5 clinger, a crippling hangover and a blistering burn, such is life: I've come to expect the unexpected.

No worry, chicken curry.

24

Woolly Mammoth

The luteal phase happens like clockwork, each month after ovulation. I become increasingly moody, anxious, and more sensitive to the world around me, on account of my right fallopian tube's recent activity. I know it's the right one because I can feel it.

It reminds me of when I tried to get into jogging. A painful stitch[21] in my side necessitated hunched over rest to catch my breath, while massaging whatever abdominal organ was spasming from the lack of oxygen.

---

[21]Apparently, this stitch during ovulation is a documented sensation called mittelschmerz. I mean, no wonder we go through it mentally, our bodies are laying eggs like hens each month.

Anyways, back to the story: I'm typing away on my laptop and my nails—that, for the record, I'm trying to grow—audibly click against the keyboard. Simultaneously, I'm aware of stray hairs tickling the back of my neck. The two sensations layer and I'm suddenly irritable, fighting the urge to stomp off to my bathroom and impulsively cut either or both. In moments like this, I truly understand why Britney shaved her head.

The high-pitched whine of a weed whacker starts up in the distance. It's rice harvesting time and the locals around these parts use the landscaping tool to cut their crops. It's a massive step up from harvesting by hand, but to my sensitive ears, the sound creates a visceral response: my shoulders hunch, my brow furrows, my jaw clenches and my breath becomes shallow.

The old fight or flight response: how incredibly unoriginal.

It's giving stone age vibes, back when our Homo sapien ancestors needed the resulting adrenaline to thwart attacks from predators, like woolly mammoths. Perhaps back then, my heightened senses would have increased my chances of survival. I alone amongst the clan, would have heard the slightest change in our environment: a twig snapping underfoot—underhoof?—I don't know; I'm not a mammoth expert, but that would be a cool profession.

As the woolly beast approached our village, I'd alert the clan to the oncoming attack and save the day. Maybe then, my sensitivities would be a gift and not a curse. Alas, in modern times I'm not at risk of mammoth tusk or woolly-hoof related injuries. As I sit in front of my laptop, the adrenaline coursing through my veins does not help my survival. It only solidifies the bulbous knots of tension in my neck and what I can only imagine are calcified adrenal glands.

The weed whacker labors and sputters an ornery mechanical squeal, making me also want to squeal, despite the time I took to sit cross-legged on the floor in silence this morning. I pause, breathing in positivity and out negativity, attempting to find neutrality over things I cannot control: the rice harvest on a Sunday morning in Ubud.

Now don't get me wrong, I'm so grateful to be in Bali. I know I'm very privileged to be in Indonesia, living in someone else's country. I respect the locals and their livelihood. My nervous system on the other hand, knows no logic.

It craves a silence so profound I'm not sure a word in the English language exists to adequately describe it. You know the kind of quiet, that's so quiet you begin to hear new sounds you didn't realize were there? For example, did you know a bird's wings make a sound as they fly? It's more of a circular whirring, than a back-and-forth flapping, and you'll only hear it in the absence of the layered noises of daily life.

Even in silence, there is still noise.

My nervous system craves a silence so silent there is nothing: a silence so thick you can nearly feel the weight and space of it; the vast emptiness of it.

But I'm afraid.

I don't think this kind of silence exists, unless I cease to exist.

Sometimes, in these moments, when I'm inundated with unwanted sound, even through the noise canceling headphones I strap on with shaking, desperate hands, I become inconsolable. The world is too loud and overwhelming, and it follows me home. Noise ricochets through the walls or windows, and the thoughts I know to be true in these moments are weighted like lead, heavy in my heart: I can't go on like this.

25

The Calm Before the Storm

I sit in front of my laptop in the detached office with its doors wide open for airflow. A soft breeze lands on my hot skin. It's not strong enough to play with the loose wisps of hair framing my face, but it's noticeable enough to hint rain is coming. It sends the seashell and coconut windchimes dangling from the roof into song.

It's the calm before the storm.

I make a very late breakfast of porridge topped with fruit, peanut butter and seeds. There's a couch at the entrance of the office where the cats nap, and I'm tempted to join them. I slump down in the space beside their fuzzy frames, gazing out into the rice field and trying to power through my oats.

I've eaten the same breakfast every day for over two years, until now. My brain suddenly sees the tiny seeds as bug eggs, and I'm revolted. I try for another spoonful, but envision insects crushing between my molars, inciting an involuntary gag reflex. I don't know why this is happening.

I struggle to replace my porridge with something else, not because I can't think of another option, but because nothing is appetizing. I have no appetite and food is just too much work—not just the grocery shopping and the cooking, but the actual chewing. I'm so turned off from food that if someone invented a pill to give me all my nutrition, I would take it indefinitely.

I know this isn't normal, but I don't know what to do about it. I'm teetering at the brink of a deep hole, knowing I could fall in at any moment.

I'm increasingly dejected to continue struggling with my mental health despite my efforts to achieve wellness. I always equated spirituality with inner peace and balance, but the deeper I dive into my journey, the more difficult it's become. I'm increasingly aware of my obsessive thoughts and the difficult emotions I tend to avoid, rather than fully feel.

Intellectually, I believe mental illness and spiritually can coexist; having mental health issues does not cancel out one's connection with God or the universe. Yet I continue to berate myself for not be 'doing it right', thinking I just need to try harder or meditate more.

I feel like I've spiritually regressed.

In part, poor integration of my transcendental spiritual practice is to blame here. According to transcendental beliefs, everything in life is neutral. Nothing is good or bad; it's our ego's attachments and aversions which dictate what we experience as good or bad. Non-attachment is therefore transcendence of our attachments and aversions.

From this perspective, my experience of disturbance from noise is not actually caused by the noise itself, but due to my aversion to sound. Noise is just an energetic vibration; it's my human mind which has attached a 'bad' or 'unpleasant' label to it.

Where this gets complicated, is when situations or stimuli are harmful. If my nervous system is wired more sensitively than others, overcoming my aversion to certain sounds is not as simple as transcending it through meditation: this would be akin to trying to meditate my eyes from brown to blue. If there's a neurological or mental reason for my sensitivity to sound, then I've unintentionally missed potential avenues of treatment in efforts of 'transcending my ego'.

As much as I initially resonated with transcendental perspectives, they're starting to fall flat as a mindfulness tool to lean on during more challenging moments. Besides, most of us aren't striving for enlightenment; we just want to feel happier and healthier in everyday life. Transcendental spiritual practices are challenging to integrate and beginners risk bypassing challenging emotions in their attempts to adopt neutrality; but suppressing is not the same as transcending. Like an iceberg, it's only a matter of time before emotions pushed below the surface cause damage.

Since arriving in Bali on my career break, my health and wellness has become my full-time job. I spend hours each day meditating and practicing yoga. I tried Balinese massage, visited a local healer and engaged in a purification ceremony. I tried a green juice cleanse, gratitude journaling, nutritional supplements and vigorous rice field walks. I dove into the new-age spiritual offerings to explore other perspectives, trying a heart chakra meditation and even a light language transmission. I removed seasonal depression from the equation by living somewhere as tropical as Bali. Despite all these things, my anxiety and noise sensitivities are only getting worse, increasingly disrupting my daily life.

Is this just part of the journey? Or is it time to admit there might be something deeper going on I'm unable to simply meditate away?

26

The Storm

I'm standing in line to place an order for takeout in Sayuri Healing Foods. I wait behind a pale, middle-aged American woman talking on a cell phone. Her pronounced Californian accent has a croaky vocal fry resembling nails on a chalkboard to my ears.

She comments on the construction noise emanating from outside: "Yeah, I'm at Sayuriiiiiii, but I'm going to have to leave…the construction is absolutelyyy unacceptable. I don't know how anyone can sit in here. It's a health hazard, a public health issue…Yeaahhh I'm just getting a smoooooo-thie."

I relate to her pain. I'm also deeply disturbed by the jack hammering in the distance, but I know construction symbolizes development and economic recovery in a post-pandemic era. It's difficult to go anywhere in Ubud these days without hearing construction, so rather than complain like this lady, I rely on my noise cancelling headphones.

The line inches towards the cashier and she hangs up her call, continuing to mutter under her breath while frantically searching for something in her canvas tote bag. I'm privy to her harshly murmured slurs and profanities:

"I'm a distinguished professional and I can't condone this mother-fucking noise pollution. It's an abomination."

My body instinctively tenses. Similar to my gut feeling with the strange man smoking under the treehouse, I sense a warning sign of danger. This lady appears unstable and I'm on-edge in her proximity.

She shakes her head and red hair frizzes at all angles like medusa. A yoga mat under her arm slides down and begins to unroll. She audibly sighs in frustration, abandoning the line to place her mat and tote on top of an empty table, continuing to dig through her bag.

I place my takeaway order and sit at the empty table next to her to wait for my food.

A young Balinese server approaches her with a smile. "Hi miss, you ready to order?"

"I just need to find my glasses. I can't remember the name of the smoothie I want, so I need a moment to read the menu."

The server doesn't fully hear her and continues, "Oh you like a smoothie?"

"I said I need a minute. Don't you people understand English?" she snaps.

I straighten up and my eyes widen in disbelief. I glance around and exchange shocked looks with other patrons across the room.

A British woman calls over from a booth, "You don't need to be so rude to her, she's just doing her job."

The Brit pauses, before doubling down. "No one here wants your bad vibes, why don't you just leave."

The American lady snaps.

She slams her hands down on the tabletop and stands up with force, stomping her way over to the Brit's table. The Balinese server retreats to the safety of her colleagues behind the counter, and they watch with faces expressing concern, shock and amusement.

"What's your name?" she demands. "I need you to write down your job title and citizenship."

I stare on in slack-mouthed shock as the confrontation unfolds in a bizarre manner closely resembling a middle-aged woman demanding to speak to a manager. She leans over the woman's table, extending her index finger directly into her face, continuing to holler.

"I was just trying to find my glasses so I could read the menu and now you're saying I'm not a citizen of this planet.

I'm from the United States of America, how dare you claim I'm not a citizen of Earth!"

It's like driving by a car crash; I'm gawking but can't look away. The American woman is visibly trembling, either on the brink of body shaking sobs or violence.

The Brit glances around the cafe, realizing all eyes are on them. "Why don't we talk outside," she offers and steps out front. The American follows her, continuing to rant about her social status as an embassy official of planet Earth and threatens to report her for war crimes.

I recognize a psychotic episode when I see one.

My takeaway order is ready and I step outside with my parcel, noticing a security guard has now joined the scene. He attempts to escort the American woman away, but she's holding her ground. She's barefoot and abandons her canvas tote bag and yoga mat on the ground. Her arms wildly undulate overhead as she continues to scream, looking as if she might throw punches at anyone who gets too close.

I make a swift getaway.

The next morning, I wake up to Neo directly on top of my chest. The largest of the three cats, he gazes down at me through narrow blue eyes, like a king on top of his throne looking upon his peasant subject. Who needs an alarm clock when you have cats?

"Good morning Big Cat," I coo while stroking his soft back. "It's time to get up now, let's get you some breakfast."

I gently lift him off me and climb out of bed, noticing another cloudy, drizzly morning in Ubud. I throw on a loose cardigan and head to the kitchen to make coffee.

Within fifteen minutes, I'm onto my second cup. Despite sleeping for ten hours, I'm exhausted. It's like other people can simply plug themselves in to recharge, rejuvenating themselves through sleep, but my 'battery' chronically exists on 'low power mode'. When I feel this way, everything is slower and five times harder.

After starting my new work contract, I reunited with old habits. I'm only contracted for part-time hours, but often work more to 'make up' for the times my brain is muddled and foggy, or too jumpy to focus. I'm unintentionally losing weight, disgusted by food or completely forgetting to eat all together.

I sit down at my laptop to start work and suddenly it's 2:00pm and I'm still in my pajamas with uncombed hair. I've not taken a sip of water or a morsel of food all day. Working from home is a slippery slope for those of us content with not leaving the house, with not changing from the same set of clothes we wore to bed, or with not speaking to another human being.

I'm also deeply disturbed by what I witnessed at Sayuri Healing Foods and can't stop thinking about the American woman. Rude behavior aside, it's obvious she was having a mental health crisis and for that, I have much compassion for her. I know what it's like to struggle mentally while living abroad, but I've never experienced psychosis or mania and can't imagine how scary it would be to have an episode so far from home.

In hindsight, I regret doing nothing. I'm unclear if interjecting myself into the situation would have helped or made matters worse, but I'm remorseful I didn't at least try, or offer to call a friend for her.

I'm abruptly shaken from my thoughts by a knock on the gate. It's a Gojek delivering another takeaway order: an easy-to-ingest soup. I return to my laptop and Neva jumps up on the desk, standing on the keys in protest for attention. My phone rings and I switch it to silent; it continues to buzz against the table. I don't have the energy to talk on the phone right now. I don't have the energy for much these days, abandoning my blog and avoiding my yoga practice.

A text comes through, "Hey, I tried to call."

I flip my phone over and attempt to refocus on work, but I'm distracted by the sound of farmers in the distance, the gurgling of the pool filter, a hammer knock-knocking, and voices from the sidewalk across the gate. The incessant sound of my own thoughts bouncing off my skull adds to the noise. They never stop by the way—the thoughts that is—they're constantly remembering, analyzing, calculating, ruminating, justifying, imagining, and looping.

Rage bubbles up inside me, inciting a visceral drumming of my heart that I hear as a steady whooshing. I sigh and get up, strapping on my noise canceling headphones to my head. They are so well used by now I'm developing a bald spot.

I turn on a mix of relaxing rainforest sounds to soothe myself and attempt to drown out the external noises that have layered and combined into one deafening 'super-sound'. It's no use; I hear it through the headphones on top of the soundtrack of chirping birds and soft rain.

A hot, prickly tear edges down my face.

I walk to the washroom and smash my shoulder off the doorframe.

My resolve shatters and I crumble. I rip the headphones off and throw them across the room, sinking to the bathroom floor.

Thud. Thud. Thud.

I'm tapping my chest, fist closed like knocking on a door, knuckles to sternum. I heard tapping is supposed to help with anxiety, a somatic release of some sort, but in my desperation, it's more forceful than necessary. I'm punching.

Thud. My fist meets my skull.

Thud. Thud. Thud. My heartbeat echoes in my ears.

Thud. My head meets the tile floor.

"You'll give yourself a concussion," a voice advises.

I hear it floating through my mind, ricocheting off the beveled ridges of my brain.

"Breathe," the tiny voice instructs, more sternly this time.

I hear it through the deafening noise, almost in the same way you can still hear sound underwater, distorted and muffled, but there nonetheless. I lift my head off the cold floor, cocking it to the side like one of the cats trying to identify the source of a clunk on the roof.

In a calm and matter-of-fact way, the voice speaks again:

"Sometimes we fall down, but we have to get back up, dust ourselves off and keep on trying."

27

The Climb

It's 3:00am and I'm standing at the edge of my street, waiting to be picked up by De. I've decided to try climbing out of the hole I've fallen into by literally climbing: De is taking me to hike Mt. Batur, Bali's active volcano.

I'm drawn to extreme sports and adventurous activities like scuba diving or mountain climbing, because they require so much focus and physical exertion it shakes me from my thoughts. The euphoria after an adrenaline activity is a celebration of life: it reminds me I'm alive and that I'm capable of doing difficult things.

We head Northeast from Ubud under the cover of darkness and arrive to the base of Mt. Batur before sunrise. I meet Made, a young Balinese guide who will accompany me to the top. We strap on headlamps to illuminate the trail and set off into the darkness.

At an elevation of 1717 meters, it's not an easy climb, especially in my sleep deprived state. Crushed volcanic stones the consistency of gravel covers the trail in a fine layer, making it slippery. An old woman with a walking stick loses her footing and slides, but her guide catches her before she falls.

My breathing is labored, but I'm determined to continue without stopping. It feels good to move my body and focus on a task so tangible and predictable: if I simply continue, with one foot in front of the other, we will make it to the top. It offers back a sense of control during a time when I feel the opposite.

We pass older hikers and groups who stop for water breaks and fifty minutes later, Made and I arrive at the top of Mt. Batur. It's still dark so there's no view, a rather anticlimactic finish to summiting a volcano. My sweat turns cold in the frigid breeze, and I huddle for warmth around a cup of coffee.

I sit in silence, looking into the vast blackness and send out a telepathic message to the divine.

For the first time in two decades, I pray.

Dear God,

It's me…Stephanie Jean Huff. Long time no talk. I know it's rude to only reach out now, when I need something, especially since it's been almost twenty years, but I hope you'll understand. I could really use your help right now.

I'm lost.

I've spent so much time traveling the world, thinking I would figure out what the point is to all of this, to life I mean, but I only have more questions. I'm exhausted and I'm angry with you; so angry I could scream. Surely you didn't create us just to suffer, so why is there so much pain in the world? Why do I have so many blessings, when others live in poverty and abuse and war? How am I supposed to sleep at night knowing this?

I want to be a better person and do good in the world…I'm trying, but I just can't seem to balance everything. If I could just figure out my mental health, I could do better. You know, like on airplanes when they tell you to put your oxygen mask on before helping others. Well, I guess you've probably never been on an airplane, but then again, you created the person who invented them, so hopefully you get what I mean.

Please guide me and give me strength to continue…but God, if you're going to send me a sign, make it obvious. If you haven't already noticed, I'm smart but sometimes oblivious…and sorry for doubting you all these years.

Oh, and please give my Grandmother a big hug for me (wait…can you hug? I guess you don't have a body. Okay never mind, tell her I'm thinking of her from down here).

With love from Bali,
Stephanie Jean

I send my prayer up to the universe, like a canang sari, a Balinese offering laid at the doorway to the cosmos and sip my coffee with gratitude for the moment unfolding before my eyes. The sun peeks out over the ridge of the volcano, illuminating the horizon in hues of golden brass, blood orange and mandarin.

De hitched a ride on the back of a motorcycle and now joins us at the top, bringing over a second mug of coffee. Sunbeams warm my face and I close my eyes.

Cheeky monkeys conveniently appear just in time for breakfast. Hikers admire the view while grazing on banana sandwiches and hard-boiled eggs. Some toss bits to the more patient apes, while more aggressive tiny beasts steal food straight from unsuspecting hiker's hands.

A dog appears in front of me and grabs at the water bottle I'm holding. He expertly unscrews the plastic cap with his teeth and slurps the rest of the liquid in greedy gulps.

"Rainbowwww!" De exclaims with surprised delight.

"That's Rainbow! Wow, he was really thirsty."

She looks from the satisfied dog, now hovering near me for affection, to my face as if appraising me.

"You are filled with light, Stephanie. What a beautiful soul you have."

I fight off the tears welling in my eyes and smile widely.

"So do you De, so do you."

She laughs and reaches for my hand.

"Come, it's time to make our way down."

28

Epilogue: Two Years Later

After six-months on the Island of the Gods, I moved onwards to Thailand. I planned to work remotely from a rental apartment in coastal Krabi, imagining weekends spent island hopping and lazing on immaculate sand beaches. Immediately after arriving though, I collapsed into an anxiety riddled state of overstimulation so deep, it neared a complete mental breakdown. I was bedridden for 5 days in another forced state of stillness via illness.

The sign I prayed for came in the form of a TikTok video.

As I lay there, bed rotting in my Thai apartment, passing time by scrolling on my phone for hours, a video gave me pause: "Signs of 'Neurodivergence' in Women." It was the remaining puzzle piece that effortlessly fit into the bigger picture of my life; the answer I'd been seeking all along.

I knew whatever was going on with my mental health was beyond meditation and 'good vibes', but I never considered I could be neurodivergent. It would explain all my issues: sensory aversions, feeling overstimulated and socially awkward without alcohol, needing to 'recover' from socialization, finding comfort in solitude and even using coffee to focus.

As a researcher by background, I dove into the medical literature and performed countless psychometric assessments on myself; the results warranted a professional evaluation. I joined a lengthy wait list and spent the next year 'in limbo', hesitant to tell anyone in my life what was going on because 'what if I was wrong'.

I wasn't wrong.

Even though it was no surprise to me by then, a formal psychological diagnosis at thirty-four is still a shock. It felt like being on board a turbulent plane, staring into the back of the leather seat with wide-eyed horror as my life took a sudden nosedive from everything I've ever known. You see, I was diagnosed with autism spectrum disorder.

I'm autistic.

Dear reader, you might be wondering how it's possible.

How could I not know?

How did no one know?

If I was diagnosed a decade earlier, I would have likely ended up with Aspergers, diagnostic terminology no longer used but still associated with 'high functioning' autism. I blame my affinity for pattern recognition, helping me to analyze, anticipate and mimic behaviors within social situations. This allowed me to blend in with my peers and colleagues—that and fifteen years of using alcohol as a social lubricant.

After five months of sobriety in Bali, my nervous system was no longer subdued by alcohol and reverted to its baseline status: hyper-sensitive. I was no longer numbing myself but as a result, I felt the full extent of my debilitating sensory issues, such as agonizing aversions to sound. My manic behavior described in the prologue was chalked up to a dual diagnosis of ADHD.

I'm not sure what's more terrifying: the realization I've spent over three decades not truly knowing myself or the blatant uncertainty which lies ahead. What I do know, is life will never be the same.

I recently read somewhere life altering things are allowed to be life altering. Like a seamstress, loosening a garment to create more room for growth, space is required to undergo personal evolution.

As scary as change is, it's the only constant we have in this life: a perpetual ebbing and flowing. With an acceptance of the utter lack of control I truly have over my life (and evidently, also over my nervous system), there is a newfound freedom unfurling its tiny wings.

My time in Bali allowed for recalibration: a rebirth of sorts. In hindsight, I often think about the backpacker legend of the magic of Bali and wonder if it's real. According to new-age spiritual beliefs, Bali reflects our own energy back to us, serving up life lessons we need to learn.

As put by one of the hippies of Ubud: "The energy here is powerful, it's like a vortex. It can elevate you to new heights or suck you up and spit you back out". I certainly feel like I was sucked up and spit back out, but for a greater purpose: to figure out my mental health.

On a later visit to Bali, I asked De if the Balinese also believe in this legend, and she said yes, summarizing it as karma: every action has a reaction. To achieve harmony in life, De says we must have a good relationship with God, other people and the environment around us—and isn't this really what we mean when we talk about 'balance'?

My spiritual journey inevitably became a healing journey and there are three things I learned along the way. The first is you can't go back; you can't return to the old version of yourself, and you can't unknow the things you now know. It can be confronting to face the older version of yourself before the new one has even fully formed. It can also be incredibly isolating because your growth will inevitably mean you outgrow certain people in your life.

The second hard lesson is healing requires facing our past wounds and traumas head on. This will involve 'growing pains' and will be extremely difficult. I always thought of spirituality as the process of finding inner peace. I didn't equate it with breakdowns on a bathroom floor, so naturally I assumed I wasn't doing it right.

If this is you my dear reader, I send you so much love and compassion. You are on the right path: it's just a challenging path; you might feel worse, before you feel better. That's why they call it 'the dark night of the soul'. Skipping over this part is only going to prolong the pain, like putting a band aid over an ailment, rather than finding its source.

The third lesson is the journey never really ends: it's iterative and cyclical. Just when we think we've figured life out, we're humbled again by it, lost and unsure which way to turn. Life is messy and the journey is winding, but maybe that's the point.

I've learned journeys are about the process, not the outcome, so naturally my inner work is not done, nor is my journey complete. I suppose this is just life: it often fails to conform to our expectations. Ironically, I spent a decade traveling the world in search of answers to my existential questions, but all this time I was looking in the wrong places. It was my inner truth I was seeking.

While I'm not retiring from travel, I am learning how to set new boundaries: what my body can and cannot tolerate, and what accommodations my nervous system requires. I still suffer from bouts of sensory overload, overwhelm and anxiety; I still have a million questions and grapple with my faith; I'm still trying to find moments of stillness.

I'm the same old me, but I'm more 'me' than the version who came before her.

I'll be honest with you dear reader, I'm not where I thought I'd be at this point in my life. It's not how I imagined it. It's both better and it's worse: the highs are higher, and the lows are lower. Yet, I have gratitude. I now know why I am the way I am, and with this raw unfolding, I see an opportunity to bloom.

Acknowledgements

I have tremendous gratitude to the island of Bali for offering a temporary home during the times I felt untethered, ultimately helping me transition from breakdown to breakthrough. My first extended stay in Bali in 2022 awakened me to the source of my mental health challenges: what I perceived as life-long anxiety was actually neurodiversity. My second visit to Bali in 2023 helped me establish a new norm after my diagnosis, where I set new boundaries and routines to prioritize my nervous system. My third extended stay on the island in 2024 fostered a new sense of self and a readiness to share my story (which ultimately turned into the writing of this book).

I would like to express gratitude to my number one fan and supporter since birth, Janis, my mom, who generously volunteered her time as the primary editor of this book. Big thanks to my dad, Tim, for his unwavering and unquestioning support of my unique journey and its ever-changing path. Much love to Jess for offering a constant ear, shoulder and verbal slap, and to my Ry for teaching me I'm lovable. Terima kasih to my friend De for answering questions and sharing about Balinese Hinduism and cultural beliefs, which supported content in this book. To everyone else who has been a part of my journey, I'm eternally grateful for your presence in my life, however brief or permanent.

Dr. Stephanie Huff is a neurodivergent Canadian researcher, writer and founder of the travel blog 'The Pink Backpack'. Her writing, which has been published in scholarly text, print and digital media, explores themes of travel, gender and health. She now advocates for women's mental health and shares her own story in her debut travel memoir, 'With Love from Bali'.

Huff grew up in London, Ontario, where she achieved a PhD from Western University before completing a postdoc in Ireland. She traveled to 60 countries while working her way around the world, prior to becoming a research consultant and published author. You can connect with her on social media @thepinkbackpack or her website: www.thepinkbackpack.com.

More from Stephanie Huff

An Excerpt from Book #2: An Indian Adventure

I've never had much appreciation for gravity, until I boarded a plane that fell from the sky.

Forty-thousand feet above, our red eye flight barrelled forward through the night at an unfathomable speed. The sheer velocity of air travel is not truly appreciated until there's turbulence, and even then, I often feign a restrained confidence to conceal my anxiety. It might be visible nonetheless: the slight downward turn of tightly pressed lips or fingers clutching an arm rest.

The plane shuddered, precariously lurching forward. My eyes flickered peripherally towards the flight attendants in attempts of reassuring myself, but to my alarm, they too looked worried. They scuttled by with the drink cart, eyes glued to the back and steadily retreating their high-heeled steps towards the safety of their own seat belts.

The plane plunged.

My stomach reached my throat, much in the same uncomfortable way it does during that initial moment a roller coaster begins to barrel down a steep plummet. Shrill screams filled the cabin, but I found myself silent. The moment seemed to be suspended, as if the clocks had stopped, as if time itself ceased to exist up there in the clouds.

Fear. Frozen. Falling.

The plane straightened out and I reached for the rose quartz crystal resting in the zipped pouch of my backpack, a gift from my best friend meant to protect me on my travels—the irony of this was not lost on me. I turned the crystal in my right hand, working it into my palm and finding comfort in the smoothness of its corners and edges.

My left hand was clutched tightly by my seatmate, a stranger whose fingers were now intimately entwined with mine. She gripped my hand in a way that gave me a new appreciation for the term 'white knuckling'. We quite literally held onto each other for dear life.

The plane violently thrashed and plummeted again, causing several overhead compartments to open and luggage to spray down like drops of rain, cueing blood curdling screams and cries from passengers as wheeled bags collided with skulls. I knew it was serious because the pilot didn't make an announcement to alleviate our collective anxiety. I accepted the graveness of our situation with unexpected neutrality.

I've lived a good life. If this is it, I've lived a good life.

My seatmate, who's name I never caught, continued to grip my hand and pray, over and over—like the crystal I turned in my palm—over and over. I don't recall whether our fingers, braided together like plaits, were perspiring. I imagine under the circumstances, they must have felt uncomfortably clammy, a juxtaposition to the bone-dry knot in my throat.

It wasn't until the plane straightened and shell-shocked flight attendants unbuckled themselves to return to their drink cart duty—a service rendered redundant in my opinion, unless they were serving liquor—that I realized I was trembling.

Now you might think this a bad omen to start a trip, just like you might have raised your eyes at the crystal I reached for in response to my own impending mortality, but I'm not so much superstitious, as I am spiritual. We all need something to believe in.

If I were to perish on an airplane careening towards the Atlantic Ocean, I'd like to believe it was fated. I'd like to think that I was meant to board that plane; that I wasn't just 'in the wrong place at the wrong time', but rather, I was destined to sit in 27A clutching the sweaty hand of a stranger. I'd like to think of myself in that moment like a shooting star, destined to fall from the sky.

The experience thrust me into the abrupt realization of the impermanence of life and that no matter how much I tried to control aspects within it, life is ultimately out of our control. My feeble future plans were no match against the force of gravity, and whatever higher presence governs our planet and beyond.

While the urgency of the situation had passed, the crystal in my palm continued to turn with vigor, like the repetitious thought in my mind.

My life is in the hands of the universe.

I'd surrendered to an unforeseen higher power, blindly entrusting and endowing my precious life to what I perhaps would never fully know or understand. I realized I was thirsty: it was an unquenchable, insatiable thirst for something I couldn't name.

I'd spend the better part of a decade wandering this Earth in search of a remedy for that thirst. It was a void I couldn't quite put my finger on, but which I acutely, viscerally, felt.

My spiritual journey had begun.

www.ingramcontent.com/pod-product-compliance
Lightning Source LLC
LaVergne TN
LVHW091934050825
817976LV00007B/149

* 9 7 8 1 0 6 8 9 5 4 0 0 9 *